r manual

THE BACKROAD

D0197885

The Backroads of Holland

Scenic Excursions by Bicycle, Car, Train, or Boat

Helen Colijn

BICYCLE BOOKS - SAN FRANCISCO

Printed in the United States of America

Published by
Bicycle Books, Inc., PO Box 2038, Mill Valley, CA 94942 (USA)

Distributed to the book trade by:
USA: National Book Network, Lanham, MD
UK: Chris Lloyd Sales and Marketing Services, Poole
Canada: Raincoast Book Distribution, Vancouver, BC

Cover design Kent Lytle, Lytle Design
Cover photograph Netherlands Board of Tourism (NBT)

All photos by the author, except as credited otherwise
Maps by Lucy Sargeant, Palo Alto, CA

Publisher's Cataloging in Publication Data
Colijn, Helen, 1920—
The Backroads of Holland: Scenic Excursions by Bicycle, Car, Train, or Boat
Series Title: The Active Travel Series.
Bibliography: p. Includes index.
1. Travel, International, Holland (The Netherlands),
2. Bicycles and Bicycling, Touring,
3. Holland
I. Title,
II. Authorship.

Library of Congress Catalog Card Number 91-77704
ISBN 0-933201-44-3 Paperback original

_____ For Maarten and Kasper

ACKNOWLEDGMENTS

Many people helped, in various ways, with the making of this book.

In Holland, these include staff members of the following organizations: Aerophoto Eelde; ANVV; ANWB; "Batavia" Lelystad; Bloemenveiling 't Noorden; Delta-Expo; Hotel Ambassade; Keukenhof; LF; Ministerie van Landbouw, Milieu Beheer, en Visserij; Museum voor Scheepsarcheologie; Nationaal Beiaardmuseum; Het Nationale Park De Hoge Veluwe; KLM; De Nederlandsche Bank; NBT; NS; NTFU; PGEM; PTT Post; RVD; SLAW; Stedelijk Museum; Stichting Oude Groninger Kerken; Thermenmuseum; all 12 provincial VVV's; many of the local VVV's; Vrienden van de Voetveren.

There were also Dutch men and women in the private sector: Frans Andringa; Annette and Bert Eykemans; Jan Hovinga; Ib Huysman; Joke Kips; Henk and Riek van Lenning; Jopie de Man; Ernst van Mackelenbergh; Thomas Maarssen, Jr.; Anneke Menger; Fons Olbertz; Ivo, Madelyn, and Titia van Rijckevorsel; Maurits van Rooijen; Bob Tromp; Gerrit Veldhorst; Gerbrand de Vries; Frits Weideman; Jan-Pieter Weijers and Mieke; Reint Wobbes. I thank them all!

In the United States, I owe a big thank you to Gerrie Davidson of the NBT in San Francisco and Peter Theunissen of The Netherlands Embassy in Washington D.C.; to Colleen Huston who assisted in preparation of the manuscript; to Robert van der Plas, my editor at Bicycle Books; and to Lucy Sargeant who drew the maps.

In last instance, I would like to thank the Americans who joined me on two Holland cycling tours: the group of 1986— Bud Coulter, Nusi Dekker, Sandy Jones, Gary Luttrell, Jack and Anne Rutherdale, Ed and Elaine Sheffield, and the group of 1987—Robyn Aye, Ken and Grace Covey, Etty Huynen, Ted and Diane Johnson, Judy Monsen, Don and Helen Walker. It was mainly because of their enthusiasm for cycling the backroads of Holland that I wrote this book.

AUTHOR'S NOTE

This book is about Holland beyond the big cities. It's about destinations in each of the 12 provinces you may like to go to once you have seen the Rembrandts, the Van Goghs, the patrician houses along the canals of Amsterdam, and the attractions of other Dutch cities usually included on a capsule tourist circuit.

The Backroads of Holland is a personal book. I write about what I like and what I think you will enjoy. Since more and more travelers are discovering that the bicycle is a fine way to tour a foreign land, you'll find ample information on cycling, including twenty one-day loop-routes which I cycled in 1990 for this book.

You'll find maps of each route I cycled and information about the train or bus I took to the starting point, the hotel in which I stayed, the place I rented my bicycle, and the map I used. All you'd have to do, if you want to follow one of my suggestions, is to make a few phone calls to reserve a rental bicycle and a room if you need them, and you can cycle away.

I chose these particular routes with the idea that if you were to ride a few, you would obtain a pretty good picture of Holland's backroads. The choice of routes was also influenced by hotel and bicycle rental availability.

However, any cycling in Holland may be far from your mind. Perhaps you have never cycled in your life, you don't feel up to it now, or you don't have the time. If any of these are the case, just skip chapter 2, the cycling information at the end of chapters 3 through 15, and chapters 16, 17, and 19. The rest of the book can be used by anyone who doesn't cycle. You can reach all points of interest I mention by car or public transport, and some by boat, in a covered wagon, or on foot as well.

I hope you will enjoy traveling the backroads of Holland with me, whether on a bicycle, by other means of transport, or even from an armchair in your home.

Helen Colijn (pronounced "Co-line") was born in England of Dutch parents, went to nursery school in California, and received her formal schooling in Holland. During her school years, she became well acquainted with the Dutch countryside, especially around her home in The Hague, both through long family walks and periodic ice skating tours. Since settling in the United States in 1946, she has returned to Holland at least once each year, further exploring the country on these visits.

Some of these excursions were personal, often undertaken with her daughter, who was raised in California and settled in Amsterdam after graduating from Amsterdam University, and lately with her two Dutch grandsons.

Other excursions were professional. Thus, she escorted American teenage girls through Holland in conjunction with her Summer-in-Europe program, or American adults on her

Cycling-in-Holland tours. At other times, she scouted travel articles for *Sunset* magazine, when she was a member of that monthly's editorial staff, and did research for her earlier book *Of Dutch Ways*, a book about Holland and the Dutch, containing chapters on history, politics, customs, cuisine, etc.

Photo by Ivo van Rijckevorsel

In the 1980's she wrote *Song of Survival—Women in a Prison Camp*. It is the inspiring story of how, during the Second World War, six hundred Dutch, British, and Australian women and children (including Helen herself) survived 3½ years of internment during the Japanese occupation of what is now Indonesia and was a Dutch colony at the time. The focus of this book is a "vocal orchestra" of thirty women who *sang* music originally written for piano and orchestra by Dvorák, Beethoven, and Chopin.

While working on *The Backroads of Holland*, Helen also wrote the text for a large format photo-essay book *Holland*, published in 1992 by Graphic Arts Center Publishing.

Today, Helen lives in a house between a redwood and a eucalyptus tree in Menlo Park, California—when she is not traveling.

TABLE OF CONTENTS

Part I

The Basics of Travel in Holland

CHAPTER 1

General Travel Information

Land of Two Names

The Dutch call their country Holland or *Nederland*—The Netherlands in English. Nederland, meaning lowland, is the country's official name. You'll find it on maps of Western Europe, bordered by the North Sea in the west and the north, by Germany in the east, and by Belgium in the south. You'll see the name Nederland, or derivations thereof, on Dutch postage stamps, coins, and banknotes.

Holland, however, is the country's popular name and goes back to the end of the 16th century. A province called Holland, now split into South Holland and North Holland, was one of the seven provinces that joined together to form the new Republic of the United Netherlands. Through international shipping and trade, the province Holland became the richest

A bridge, a river, and a few of Holland's two million dairy cows make up a very Dutch landscape.

and most powerful. The outside world began referring to the entire republic as Holland and continued to do so even after the republic became the Kingdom of The Netherlands in 1813. The country is now divided into twelve provinces: Drenthe, Flevoland, Friesland, Gelderland, Groningen, Limburg, North Brabant (*Noord Brabant* in Dutch), North Holland (*Noord Holland*), Overijssel, South Holland (*Zuid Holland*), Utrecht, and Zeeland, in alphabetical order.

In most tourist publications you will find the provinces grouped by geographical location as follows: Groningen, Friesland, Drenthe (the northern provinces); Overijssel and Gelderland (the eastern provinces); Flevoland; Utrecht; North Holland, South Holland, and Zeeland (the maritime provinces); North Brabant and Limburg (the southern provinces).

In the 20th century, the new breed of Dutch image makers deliberately chose to call the country Holland. They said—and who will deny it—that The Netherlands sounds ponderous and dull, while Holland sounds lively and happy. Goods now go out into the world with a label "Made in Holland," KLM Royal Dutch Airlines advertise themselves as "Holland's Reliable Airline," and the Netherlands Board of Tourism, or NBT, promotes Holland.

Small-Scale Country

Holland is only 120 kilometers (72 miles) east to west through the middle, and 300 kilometers (180 miles) north to south. (If the conversion from kilometers to miles baffles you, see Appendix D.) Nearly everything in this small country matches its size. The highest mountain, the Vaalserberg in the province of Limburg, rises only 322 meters, less than 1000 feet above *normaal Amsterdams peil*, the level of ground water in Amsterdam against which the Dutch measure altitudes and depths. The biggest city, Amsterdam, has 700,000 inhabitants. America's biggest city, New York, has 14 million—almost as much as the total population of The Netherlands, which is 15 million. What Dutch tourist brochures enthusiastically call extensive forests are puny compared to national forests in Canada or the United States.

You may well find that this small scale is part of Holland's charm. As you travel through the countryside, wooded areas, heaths, marshes, lakes, rivers, canals, cultivated fields, pastures, villages, and towns pass by in quick succession. You don't have a chance to get bored. And amid all this small-scale scenery lie truly impressive and often large-scale works, testimonies of Holland's struggle against the water: high-tech river sluices that stop rivers from flooding the land, a dam so long you can't see the end when you start off on it, big chunks of land that were reclaimed from the sea and reach as far as the horizon. (These pieces of land are *polders*, dike-surrounded areas where the water level can be controlled by old-time windmills or electric and steam-powered pumps. You'll find information about the makings of polders in chapters 4, 7, and 10.)

"Randstad:" **Rim City**

The *Randstad*, or Rim City, is the heavily urbanized area in the West that embraces Holland's four major cities. They are Amsterdam, the nation's capital, in the province of North Holland; The Hague, residence of the royal family and seat of the national government, in the province of South Holland; Rotterdam, home of a huge international port, also in South Holland; and the city of Utrecht in the province of Utrecht.

Postage stamp showing Holland's current Queen Beatrix and her three predecessors, Juliana, Wilhelmina, and Emma. (Photo courtesy PTT Post)

Much of Holland's varied scenery lies in the outer provinces,but you can find characteristic Dutch scenery right in Rim City too. When the fast-growing area risked blending into one huge conglomeration, the Dutch judiciously designated green buffer zones between the cities and preserved some of the landscapes.

Talking About the Weather

Although Holland lies as far north as the Canadian province of Newfoundland, the marine climate generally translates into mild winters and cool summers. Winter temperatures are likely to hover around the freezing point. Skies are gray and somber. Fog may blanket roads. But some winters the temperatures drop way down, canals and lakes freeze over, and the Dutch skate on the ice. Skies may then be a pure crisp blue. Summer temperatures fluctuate around 20°—25° Celsius (69°—77° Fahrenheit). Summer temperatures occasionally rise past 25° Celsius and the Dutch talk about a heat wave. Daytime temperatures in spring and fall range from 5° to 15° Celsius (40° and 60° Fahrenheit) during the day.

As for rain, there is no pattern: rains may come in short bursts alternated with sunshine, in dreary drizzles for several days or even weeks, or may be absent for days or weeks at a time. Pack a raincoat or an umbrella and hope that you'll be blessed with a spell of fine dry days. Every season has its share. For a weather forecast in English, updated four times a day, dial 06–320 328 31, although this service may be discontinued.

When to Go

Do you want to stay only in cities, to enjoy museums, restaurants, theaters, dance clubs, and bars? And will you be traveling by train? If so, winter could be a good time, and you wouldn't run into masses of other tourists. Or do you also, or exclusively, want to tour the country's backroads? In that case, other times of the year would be more suitable. My own choices for backroads travel, particularly on a bicycle, are April, May, June, and September.

April may still be chilly (you'll need woolen gloves on the bicycle) with even a day of wet snow or hail. *"April doet wat hij wil,"* say the Dutch, April does what it wants. But in April the influx of foreign tourists hasn't gathered momentum and it's usually easy to find overnight accommodations. After mid-April, in most years, Holland begins bursting out in blooms. All over the country, along city streets, in private gardens, and in parks, bushes and trees flower—cherry, apple, magnolia, hawthorn, chestnut, and rhododendron—one kind after another or at the same time right through the end of May.

Also in April the fields of tulips, daffodils, and hyacinths, many of them in Rim City, begin spreading their carpets of red, yellow, and blue blooms. The public Keukenhof gardens near Haarlem display a wondrous collection of flowering bulbs. Just when the "bulb season" starts and ends depends on the weather of the previous months, but the peak is usually between mid-April and mid-May.

May is usually warmer than April. More foreign tourists are now in Holland because of the tulips, but they often come for short trips and stay only in Rim City. During the bulb season it may be hard to find on short notice exactly the accommodations you want there. June is generally warmer than May and less crowded. The tourists who came for the tulips are gone and the summer season hasn't started. The Dutch with school-age children aren't vacationing yet— schools are still in session. July and August are the top foreign tourist months.

Throughout Holland, thousands of these mushroom-shaped signs guide cyclists and hikers. (see page 32)

19

In summer you should reserve accommodations well ahead. The same goes for long weekends that precede the summer: four-day Easter weekend (Good Friday, a national holiday, Saturday, Easter Sunday, Easter Monday, also a national holiday), four-day Ascension Day weekend, starting a Thursday 40 days after Easter, or Whitsun weekend (Saturday, Whit Sunday, Whit Monday, a national holiday). Whitsun, or Pentecost, is 7 weeks after Easter. The Queen's official birthday, April 30, is also a national holiday and may create another long weekend. (Beatrix's real birthday is January 31, not a good date for elaborate outdoor celebrations.) Other feast days celebrated abroad may bring in more tourists. The days around May 1, "Labor Day," bring tourists to Holland from as far away as Italy. The French celebration of July 14th or other countries' observation of Mary's Assumption on August 15 may also be felt in Holland.

In September most of the foreign tourists are gone, and it's easy again to find overnight accommodations on the spur of the moment. The weather still carries with it some of the summer's warmth.

How to Reach Holland

If you are in Great Britain, you can reach Holland by taking a daily ferry boat from Sheerness in England to Vlissingen (Flushing), from Harwich to Hoek van Holland, from Great Yarmouth to Scheveningen, or from Hull to Rotterdam. Ferries also sail to Holland, although not on a daily basis, from Bergen in Norway and Gothenburg in Sweden. If you come from the U.S., Canada, or countries other oceans away , you'll have to fly.

More than 80 different airlines currently fly into Amsterdam's Schiphol airport, often called *Skiphol* because the Dutch guttural "ch," also spelled "g," is difficult to pronounce for most other people.

During the more than 40 years I've been commuting between California and The Netherlands, I've always flown KLM Royal Dutch Airlines. My choice is prompted by convenience: KLM flies directly from Los Angeles to Amsterdam (as it does from several other U.S. gateways) and arrives in Holland in the afternoon. I find this preferable to morning arrival in view of jet lag, and fares and service are on a par with, or better than, those of competing carriers.

Local Sources of Information

To find out ahead of arrival what Holland has to offer, call or write to the office of the Netherlands Board of Tourism (NBT) nearest to you (see Appendix A).

In Holland, look for one of the 400 VVV's, pronounced in Dutch *Vay-Vay-Vay*. The three V's stand for *Vereniging voor Vreemdelingenverkeer*, which translates as Association for Travel by Visitors. Since many of those visitors are Dutch, printed tourist information may only be in Dutch, but English-speaking VVV hosts or hostesses can tell you about amusement parks, casinos—there are 8 in Holland—, castles, churches with famous organs, concerts, craft fairs, hotels, museums— Holland has more than 800—, sporting events, theatrical performances, or train and ferry schedules anywhere in the country. You can pick up free folders and brochures and buy guide books and maps. For a small fee, VVV's make reservations for hotels and theaters, provided these are listed in their electronic file. Inquire which days of the week VVV's, sights, and shops will be closed.

ANWB Royal Dutch Touring Club

Another good source for travel information in Holland is the touring club ANWB. The letters stand for *Algemene Nederlandsche Wielrijders Bond*, or General Dutch Cyclists Association, the club's name at birth more than 100 years ago, before the invention of the automobile. You must be a member of an auto-club that belongs to the AIT, Alliance Internationale de Tourisme, to receive ANWB information, so bring your auto-club card even if you will be traveling without a car. AA and

RAC in the United Kingdom, AAA in Australia, CAA in Canada, and AAA in the U.S. are all AIT members and sister organizations of the ANWB.

VVV Maastricht celebrated its move to a 500-year-old building with a large VVV logo on a banner.

ANWB guest privileges allow you to receive travel information at any of 50 or so ANWB offices. There you can also buy travel-related items such as a day-pack or a multiple electric plug (for use in any country where the voltage is 120-220), and a large array of ANWB maps. You can also buy, at a slightly higher price, ANWB maps at VVV offices or at the specialized travel bookstores mentioned in Appendix A.

One ANWB map you may like is the 1:300,000 road map of The Netherlands with legends in Dutch and 3 other languages including English (British English, so freeway appears as dual carriageway). A place name register is on the back.

You'll probably be enchanted by the ANWB 1:100,000 sectional *toeristenkaarten*, tourist maps that cover the country in 14 sheets. You'll see where the heaths are (pink), woods (green), water (blue), sand dunes (yellow), built-up areas (brown), and all the freeways, highways, and byways (the thin yellow lines of the backroads). Also shown are all the bicycle paths and footpaths, symbols for areas with signed walking routes, symbols for tourist attractions from prehistoric graves to windmills, and the numbers of ANWB signposts and *paddestoelen*, "mushrooms." The latter are low-placed roadmarkers for hikers and cyclists: stop at such a mushroom or signpost, compare its number with the number on your map, and you will know whether you are where you want to be. A taller mushroom, which is also readable from a car window, is now under discussion.

The ANWB tourist maps are uniform for the entire country. (This is not true of some other kinds of sectional maps.) The legends are only in Dutch, so I have translated one in Appendix C. The maps are updated every 2 to 3 years. In 1991 a map cost 8.50 guilders at ANWB, 10 guilders elsewhere in Holland.

The Currency

The guilder is the Dutch monetary unit. It is written as f, or f., or fl., abbreviations of the French word florin which means guilder, or once in a while, as Dfl., Hfl., or even Gld. A guilder is divided into 100 cents. With the steady decrease of the value of the money, cents as coins are now extinct. Dutch coins currently in use are: *Stuiver* (5 cents), *Dubbeltje* (10 cents), *Kwartje* (25 cents), *Gulden*, or guilder (100 cents), *Rijksdaalder* (2 guilders and 50 cents), and *Vijfje* (5 guilders). Beware, the 5-guilder coin has the same diameter (not the same thickness or color) as the 1-guilder coin. Don't mistake one for the other.

Dutch banknotes each have a different color and design as well. The 5-guilder note is 7 centimeters high and 13 centimeters wide (3 inches by 5 inches). The width of the notes increases by millimeters as the value increases.

The best places to change your currency or travelers checks are bona fide banks or a Grenswisselkantoor, GWK, which are open on Saturdays and Sundays. You'll find GWK counters at important border crossing points (*grens* means border), at Schiphol, and at larger train stations. Hotels and shops will also exchange your money, but at a less attractive rate.

The Language

Many Dutch speak at least some English, particularly the younger generation. English is now a compulsory subject in nearly all high schools.

Periodically, a law is passed changing the official spelling of Dutch words, so you may come upon two different spellings of the same word; for example, woods can be *bos* (new spelling) or *bosch* (with silent ch, old spelling) as in the name Biesbos or Biesbosch, a national park. Such a change won't hamper you finding the name on a map. Truly confusing, for many Dutch as well, is the place of the diphthong "ij" in an alphabetical listing. The "ij" follows the i, or it takes the place of the y, i.e. before the z. The "ij" is now often written as a y, so van Dijk appears as van Dyk.

Weights and Measures

You're likely to get by nicely without a word of Dutch, but when you go shopping you'll have to figure out the metric system of weight and measures if you are not already familiar with it. For help with this, see Appendix D.

Hotels

All Dutch hotels are classified by the Benelux hotel classification system, ranging from five-star (deluxe) to one-star (modest). Dutch organizations like ANWB and NBT also use this classification system. NBT offices abroad will send you their annual hotel guide for a nominal fee to cover postage and handling. NBT can also send you information on budget and gourmet hotels; *trekkershutten,* which are log cabins for up to four persons with no heat (bring sleeping bag and cooking gear); bungalow parks, where you rent a cottage with housekeeping facilities and can take meals in a park restaurant; and youth hostels and campsites.

You can make reservations for hotels and *trekkershutten* before you leave home through the Netherlands Reservation Centre (see address in Appendix A). You'll receive a written confirmation, but allow several weeks, unless you go the FAX route. You don't pay a reservation fee, but the hotel may ask for a credit card guarantee to hold your room. Give your credit card number and expiration date. Most credit cards are accepted. Hotels that belong to an international chain of high-priced hotels probably have a toll-free telephone reservation number in your own country.

Signs indicating some of the options for eating out (see page 26)

Included in the hotel rate, except in some expensive hotels, is breakfast. This is usually served buffet-style, at which you can help yourself to different kinds of breads and toppings, like sliced cheese or meats, honey, jams, or other types of sweet spreads in individual cups. Some hotels include fresh orange juice, dry cereals, milk, yoghurt, sausage, and scrambled eggs, but others will charge you extra for these. A soft-boiled egg that you will find under a cover in a basket is always included. Coffee and tea are on the buffet or served at your table. The plastic container you may find here is for disposal of the paper or plastic cups or bags your butter, margarine, sweet spreads, or cereal came in.

Bed-and-breakfast arrangements are best made once you are in Holland. To date no national list nor reservation system exists; VVV's may have a list of bed-and-breakfast accommodations in their province.

Restaurants

The variety of restaurants in Holland is as great as that of hotels, from a 15th-century castle with real candles in lusters hanging from a beamed ceiling to a franchise of an American hamburger chain.

Restaurants in the more expensive price range may display signs announcing that Michelin rated them with one or two stars, or that they belong to the Alliance Gastronomique Néerlandaise, which advertises "gastronomy without compromise." Some restaurants in a moderate price range belong to the Neerlands Dis Foundation with a red, white, and blue soup tureen logo. They serve delicious fresh Dutch dishes, according to a list of member restaurants that you can buy at VVV's.

Farther down the financial scale, many restaurants serve, along with other fare, a tourist menu, advertised by a blue shield with a white fork that has a camera dangling from the prongs and a hat with a flower sitting atop. Each year a fixed price is set for a three-course menu and participating restaurants serve what they wish at that price. In 1991 the tourist menu cost f. 19.50. Ask a VVV for the free Tourist Menu booklet.

Many other restaurants serve good food for all tastes and pocketbooks, including ethnic restaurants such as Indonesian, serving the cuisine of Holland's former colony. There you can eat *rijsttafel*, rice with numerous spicy side dishes, or *nasi goreng*, fried rice with only a few side dishes.

Restaurants are required by law to post sample menus and prices outside. This will help you decide whether to go in, if Dutch friends haven't already tipped you off where they like to eat. It is not unusual to receive a plate with fish filet or pork chop accompanied by a battery of dishes with 2 different vegetables, 2 different kinds of potatoes, and a salad. If you are a small eater, you could ask the waiter ahead of time what comes with your entree and ask to omit some of the choices. The custom of the "doggie bag," of taking uneaten food home, has not caught on in Holland.

Fast-food places are plentiful. Typically Dutch is a small shop, usually with a few tables, that sells freshly made *broodjes*, buttered rolls with generous servings of cheese, cold meats, and other savory toppings you point to on a counter. A *broodje croquet* means a roll or slice of bread with a small mass of minced meat coated with bread crumbs and deep-fried while you wait. Some shops use more meat in their croquettes than others. You can also often purchase French fries at these places with a big blob of mayonnaise, if you wish.

Telephone and Facsimile

If hotels take a higher commission for money exchanges than a bank does, they also charge more for telephone calls than the Dutch PTT does. The initials stand for *Post, Telegraaf, Telefoon*, 3 services combined in the newly privatized postal service.

Telephone charges for calls placed in hotels can be exorbitant. If you are on a tight budget, go to the post office or use a public telephone. At the post office you fill in a slip and render it to a clerk who assigns you a booth. Upon completion of the call you pay the amount required. To use a public telephone you need kwartjes and guilders or the recently introduced prepaid PTT calling card, the *telefoonkaart*. Slip this piece of plastic, instead of coins, into a new-style telephone and dial the number. When you talk, you will see in a little window on the phone that the number of *eenheden* (units) diminishes. When the number reaches zero, take the card out, toss it in the *afvalbak* under the telephone, insert a new card, and continue talking.

Buy a PTT card at a post office or railroad station. The cards come in denominations of 5, 10, or 25 guilders. Each unit represents 25 cents, the usual charge for a unit on a coin phone. It is virtually impossible to see on a partially used card how many units are left. Slip it into the new-style telephone, dial any existing number and watch, when you are connected, the number of units that appear in the little window (hang up before someone answers!)

When you make a telephone call inside Holland, remember to wait for the dial tone after the area code (the first 3 digits of the telephone number, such as 020 for Amsterdam, 010 for Rotterdam). When you phone to a location outside Holland, dial 9, wait for the dial tone, then, without stopping, dial the country code, the area code without the 0, and the subscriber number. You can do all this dialing directly from a public telephone, if you have enough coins in your pockets or enough units on your plastic telephone card. Instructions in English are posted on the telephone. It is often cheaper to call from the U.S. to Holland than from Holland to the U.S. because of lower rates at certain hours or other telephone company discounts in the U.S.

Before leaving home, American visitors may want to inquire from their long-distance telephone company what provisions it has for calling the United States from abroad. AT&T, for example, will give you a toll-free telephone number in the country you'll be calling from. This number connects you directly with an operator in the United States. You tell the person the number in the U.S. you want to call and your calling card number. You are charged for the call (plus a service charge) at your home or business phone at prevailing U.S. rates.

When phoning overseas from a Dutch friend's home, you can't say "let me know how much the call cost when your bill comes in and I'll reimburse you," as we often do in the U.S. because Dutch telephone bills are not itemized. It's possible to work out the charges incurred by keeping track of the minutes you talked and figuring out the sum of your indebtedness—applicable rates are in the telephone book — but much better simply to place a collect call or charge it to your credit card.

Most hotels have facsimile numbers and can send a fax for you, usually for a fee, or you can send it from the post office.

Getting Around in Holland

You can tour Holland on your own by car, train, bus, streetcar, bicycle, in a boat, covered wagon, or afoot. The last four modes

Issued in 1989, this 25-guilder note has an avant-garde design and the customary tactile labels for the visually handicapped. (Photo courtesy De Nederlandsche Bank)

are subjects of separate chapters. Below are pointers about driving, riding the train, and other public transportation.

By Car

If you come from overseas and choose to drive, this will probably be in a rental car. You can arrange for it through an international car company before you leave home, upon arrival at Schiphol airport, or at your Dutch hotel. To shop for rental prices once you are in Holland, ask a VVV for a list of local car rental companies or look in the yellow telephone book, *"De Gouden Gids."* Sometimes car rental companies do not have cars with automatic transmission. An international driver's license is not necessary for a tourist visit. The price of gasoline is likely to be several times higher than in the U.S.

Traffic rules in Holland are mostly the same as elsewhere in Europe. One Dutch rule you should be aware of is *"Rechts gaat voor,"* meaning yield to traffic from the right. The Dutch tend to barrel ahead when they have the right of way. "In Holland *'Rechts gaat voor'* is more the gospel than 'God is love,'" is a Dutch saying. This rule does not apply to cyclists, however, including people on a *bromfiets*, or *brommer* (moped in English): motor vehicles have the right of way over cyclists and moped riders in these situations. White parallel ('zebra') stripes on a street indicate a pedestrian crossing. Although drivers are supposed to stop when you walk across such a zebra crossing, you should not count on it.

Special rules are in force at a *rotonde*, roundabout as the British call it, traffic circle in the U.S. Traffic approaching the circle has the right of way, but, counsels the ANWB, the number of traffic circles is increasing where traffic driving in the traffic circle has the right of way. This is particularly true in border areas where Holland has adapted its rules to those of the neighboring country. Watch the signs. On a *rotonde* you may overtake on either side. (On a road you may only overtake on the left.)

Dutch traffic signs are the same as those in use in the rest of multilingual Europe, where the designers relied on pictograms, understandable to all, rather than words in a nation's own language. Instead of the words CHILDREN AT PLAY, there is a picture of children, instead of the words BIKE LANE, a picture of a bicycle. Triangular signs bordered in red indicate a danger. White round shields with a red border indicate who the roadway is *not* for. Blue round shields indicate for whom the roadway *is*.

On a road map you'll find numbered E-roads (part of the European freeway network, green shield), numbered A-roads (national freeways, red shield), numbered N-roads (national highways, yellow shield, and secondary roads, usually provincial roads that go by names. On the ANWB maps the secondary roads are represented by yellow lines. Follow them if you are not pressed for time and want a true backroad experience. An intersection of freeways is called *knooppunt* and shown with that word and the *knooppunt's* name on the map. Also listed on the map are the names of freeway exits that are not level. In future, exits will also receive a number. The Dutch word for exit is *afrit*. Another Dutch word you may come across is *ring* for a peripheral road around a city (Amsterdam and Rotterdam have them). Exits from a ring are numbered, e.g. *Afrit 3*.

The information on your map is, of course, also given as you drive, on overhead or roadside signs. The farthest point of a particular Dutch road will be last on the shield. Say you are going north from Amsterdam on the E 22. You see as last name on a shield Leeuwarden in the province of Friesland, way up north. If you only want to go to Hoorn, in the same province you are in, you won't see the name on a sign until you are close to the turnoff, so be sure to consult a good road map.

It's the ANWB that for nearly 100 years has been putting up signs all over Holland at the request of whoever is responsible for the road: the department of traffic and state of the water, for national roads; the provincial councils for provincial roads; or the municipal councils for municipal roads. In a country of many administrative bodies that are autonomous and like to do their own thing on their own turf, having one (private) organization that takes care of everybody's signs makes for a welcome national uniformity.

You'll see ANWB signs that announce, among other things, campgrounds and other recreational areas, hexagonal *toeristische* (scenic) route signs, provincial border signs, airport signs, river and canal signs, and signs with the names of the village you are entering. This last is sometimes followed with the abbreviation gem. and another name. Gem. stands for *gemeente* (municipality), an administrative unit that may consist of several villages; for example you might see Hoofddorp/Gem. Haarlemmermeer.

At the time of writing, the speed limits were 120 km/h (72 mph) on freeways, 100 km/h (62 mph) on regular highways, 60 or 80 km/h (37 and 50 mph, respectively) on other roads outside built-up areas. Watch the road signs. However, as in other parts of the world, the speed limits are ever subject to political discussions and may have changed when you reach Holland. You'll notice that not all Dutch pay attention to them.

Along many of Holland's freeways and highways you'll see every 2 kilometers, preceded by small black triangles at the side of the road, a yellow emergency telephone of the ANWB Wegenwacht. This is what the Dutch call a *praatpaal*, literally a speaking pole, or callbox. You pull a knob on the phone and are connected with the nearest ANWB Road Patrol station. If you are not near a *praatpaal*, call toll-free 06-0888 from a regular phone any time. State the number of the ANWB emergency telephone you are calling from, the nature of your problem, and whether you are a member of ANWB with Wegenwacht coverage (an insurance that most of ANWB's 3 million members carry), or of a sister organization that has guest privileges. In the first case the driver/mechanic of the yellow ANWB automobile that has come to your rescue will not charge for breakdown assistance or for towing by an outside service, should this be necessary. In the second case you may receive breakdown assistance free of charge, but pay for the towing depending which foreign club you belong to. If you don't qualify for any free service, or can't show a card to prove that you do, you pay a flat sum for whatever you need; in 1991 the cost was f 125.

If you plan to drive on major roads, particularly those in Rim City, it's useful to find out what the expected traffic patterns are so that you can avoid what the Dutch call *file rijden*, driving in a *file* (pronounced fee-leh), meaning a traffic jam. Newscasters give the statistics over the radio: "... 8 kilometers *file* on the A 12 near ... 6 kilometers *file* on the ... bridge." The

This NS railroad station in Weert is unusual because of its tower and asymmetrical facades.

traffic reports cover the nation and, some days, when you total all the *files* you arrive at a whopping 100 kilometers—almost the width of the country. Holiday traffic, especially on the last day of a four-day weekend, may be worse than weekday rush-hour traffic. Also be aware of football matches, pop concerts, flowering tulips, and other events that draw masses of tourists to the same place.

Parking in the big cities may also bring delays—and costs. In Amsterdam downtown, free street parking is hard to find and parking garages are costly. Metered parking can also be expensive. At some meters you may park for up to eight hours at a cost of 1 guilder for 20 minutes. Not only could this make a dent in your budget, you need a lot of coins in your pocket to feed the meter. If you overstay or park in a forbidden place, the police swiftly block your car with a *klem*, known as a 'Denver boot' in the US, on one of the wheels, or tow it away.

By Streetcar, Municipal Bus, or Taxi

In Amsterdam, as in any other Dutch city, streetcar and bus service is frequent. You will need a national *strippenkaart*, blue for adults or pink (reduced rate) for children and seniors. Fold the card over to the number of strips required for the distance you want to travel and have it stamped by the driver, or stamp it yourself in one of the yellow machines inside the streetcar (the machines are not in the buses). You can buy the blue cards from the driver, and the blue and pink ones at railroad stations, post offices, tobacco shops, and other places that have the word *strippenkaarten* posted in the window.

Taxis are stationed at the airport, near railroad stations, and at taxi stands in town. You usually cannot hail a taxi in Holland as it cruises by, but you can phone one to come and pick you up. The tip is included in the metered fare, but a little extra is expected if the driver has to haul luggage in and out of the trunk. Four passengers is the taxi limit. A ride to Schiphol airport from an Amsterdam address cost about 50 guilders in 1991. For a few guilders you can travel between the airport and Amsterdam by streetcar/train. If you have to watch your budget, avoid taking a taxi during rush hours: the meter keeps ticking away while the taxi is stalled in a traffic jam.

By Train or Regional Bus

As an alternative to the car, there is the train. You have to balance one against the other. With a car you can go from door to door, you never have to carry luggage, and you usually arrive at your destination more quickly than with public transportation. Small children may fall asleep in a car and become less tired than if they have to traipse behind you up and down train station stairs and wait at a street corner for a bus. But you do run the risk of being stuck in a traffic jam or, in a city, going around and around to find a parking place. You also have to find your own way.

In the train you can sit quietly and look out of the window, read a book, and buy a cup of coffee from the man or woman with the rolling minibar. You don't have to get worked up about other people's driving habits, the unfamiliar road signs, or the weather.

If you are 3 or more in a party, it will cost less per person per kilometer to travel in a car than in a train. Otherwise, take the train.

Now is a good time to ride the trains in Holland. The state-owned Nederlandse Spoorwegen, Netherlands Railroads, or NS, as the Dutch call them, are working hard to lure the Dutch out of their automobiles into the train. The NS is urging ticket sellers and train conductors to be *klantvriendelijk* (customer-friendly), sprucing up stations with more pictograms and restaurants, and adding new train material, additional travel discounts, and a very popular train-taxi service.

The pictograms, white designs on blue shields, are those in use elsewhere in western Europe. The picture of a suitcase and a key leads you to a baggage locker; the picture of a flower points to a florist's stall, a frequent presence at NS stations. A blue 'i' in a white circle guides you to an NS Information booth, usually in the central hall of a major train station. (Ticket sellers will also give train information but would rather not when a line of passengers is waiting behind you.) Big yellow placards in the station hall and on platforms list departure times of trains, always with the 24-hour clock, and numbers of pertinent platforms. A change in platform for an arriving or departing train is announced over the public address system. Announcements are also made in English if they concern international trains, so if you think an announcement only in Dutch might concern the train you're waiting for, look for an NS person, identifiable by the NS logo, or ask another train traveler what the Dutch announcement was all about.

A new kind of train car is the doubledecker used on some lines of the Intercity. This fast train connects some 40 Dutch cities, usually every half hour from 7:00 to 19:00. The *stoptrein* stops at every small place that rates an NS station. Schiphol also has an NS station at which you can board a train and reach any other NS station, sometimes without changing trains at all. There are nearly 400 NS stations in the country.

The equipment for first and second class is often almost the same, but second class wil be more crowded than first class, particularly during the rush hours. First class cars may also have a small section of compartments for 6 passengers, instead of the usual long cars with airline type seating or other multiple seat arrangements. At least one of these first class compartment windows will feature a picture of a man putting a finger to his lips and the words '*Stilte, Werkcoupé*' (Quiet, Working Compartment). Second class is noisier than first, but there's more to observe: high school or university students, mothers with children, working men and women of all ages, retirees, and travelers with luggage who arrived in Schiphol and boarded an NS train right at the airport.

As for ticket discounts, if you travel with young children, up to 3 years old they travel free, between 4 and 11 they travel any distance on a *railrunner* ticket that costs 1 Dutch guilder for a day. No more than 3 children per accompanying adult are allowed. If you travel with teenagers or other adults in a group up to 6, you can benefit from a *meer man's kaart*, literally a card for more men. Each person in the group pays less than if he or she were paying for a ticket separately—savings increase with a higher number in the group. However, to enjoy this reduction you must wait weekdays until 9:00 to start your train travel.

If you plan long rides within a week, consider the week pass, with no time restrictions. When you buy it at the ticket counter, you will also be issued a free NS base card for which you will need a passport photo. An "instant photo" cubicle is probably at the station. For longer stays in Holland, you may want to look into buying the *Rail-Aktief* card, if you are 26–59 years old, and the *60+* card if you are 60 or over. Both of these cards are valid for a year and entitle you to 40 percent off on all train tickets as long as you travel after 9:00 on weekdays. In 1990 the cost was 120 guilders for the *Rail-Aktief* and 80 for the *60+*. The latter card grants seniors an extra bonus: 7 days a year free travel anywhere in the country in second class, and for 10 guilders in first class.

If you are a wheelchair traveler, you can call 030-331253 Monday through Friday 8:00 to 16:00 and ask for someone to help you to the right platform and into the train. Call at least one-and-a-half days ahead of traveling time since such assistance is not available at all stations nor at all times.

The *trein taxi* will be waiting near a sign at the railroad station and for 5 guilders will take you to a local address in 50 or more places. You must buy the taxi voucher when you buy your train ticket. You can also prepay the return taxi. The NS subsidizes the taxi service. Five guilders is about where an ordinary taxi rate starts. You may have to wait for a *trein taxi* to arrive back at the station or for more passengers to arrive, but, if all goes well, no more than 10 minutes.

A number of regional bus companies work closely with the NS to offer buses that leave from train stations to places not served by the railroads. You can use your *nationale strippenkaart* to pay. Virtually every village in The Netherlands without a railway station is served by a *streekbus* (regional bus), most of which run at least once an hour. Schedules may be reduced on Sundays. It helps to relax and not feel hurried when using the regional bus system.

Each year the NS prints up a number of free booklets in Dutch to explain services and discounts to the country's train travelers. The Intercity timetable includes an explanation in

Sections of the Nationale Strippenkaart are cancelled to pay the fare in busses or streetcars all over the country. Fold the card at the appropriate line and insert in the cancellation device.

English. For sale are the *Spoorboekje*, the railway time table, listing all train connections in the country, and the *Nationale Buswijzer*, with information on the 16 regional bus services. After May 31, 1992, you will be able to dial 06-9292, the number of *OV (Openbaar Vervoer) Reisinformatie*, Public Transportation Travel Information, and find out from an English-speaking operator how to travel from door to door anywhere in the country. Information will relate to municipal streetcar or bus, train, regional bus, or combination thereof.

CHAPTER 2

Cycling Information

If you are not already a cycling enthusiast, you may become one in Holland, a country with 10,000 kilometers (6,000 miles) of bicycle paths, most of them flat. On these paths, the Dutch cycle to school, to work, to the post office, to the market, and to relatives and friends. When there are no bicycle paths, they cycle on the roads, mingling unperturbed with cars and other four-wheel vehicles. It's estimated that every weekday some 4 million Dutch (out of the country's 15 million) ride bicycles for utility. On a weekend or holiday with suitable weather, huge numbers of Dutch cycle for recreation.

Cycling in Holland

Cycling has much to recommend it, apart from all those mostly flat paths to ride on. In this small-scale country you're never far from human habitation and a telephone if, for example, you have a flat tire and don't know how to fix it or forgot to bring a tire repair kit. And you're never far from a café or a food shop,

Cycling on a bikeway in the coastal dunes near Noordwijk, far away from traffic noise and fumes. (Photo courtesy VVV Noord Holland)

although on Sundays all shops and, in some areas of the country, all cafés are closed. On a bicycle you're much more free to go where you want than in a car. You can also more easily stop to savor the landscape, take photos, consult a map, or ask a local person for the way.

The drawbacks of cycling in Holland could be the rain and the wind. As mentioned in the previous chapter, it does rain in Holland throughout the year, intermittently and unpredictably. There isn't much you can do about wind, other than charting a route with the direction of the wind in mind (check in the morning paper). Do not, for example, cycle the 32-kilometer dam that closes off the Zuiderzee in an eastern direction when an east wind blows. Be sure to avoid being buffeted by a head wind on top of dikes, which are always higher than the surrounding land (although mercifully many dike roads are lined with trees). If you are cycling a loop and cannot, therefore, avoid headwinds some of the time, try to take on the headwinds in a wooded area if there is one nearby. In a pinch, cycle a route with the wind in your back and return by train. There are also days with only the whisper of wind or no wind at all. If, however, the mere idea of cycling against the wind already bothers you, then cycling in Holland is probably not for you.

Types of Bicycle Paths

You'll be cycling on two basic types of paths:
- ☐ Roadside bicycle paths. These run parallel to motor roads, often well separated from them by a row of trees or a *sloot*, a small drainage canal, and are primarily utilitarian paths.
- ☐ Bikeways. These bicycle paths veer off solo into polders, sand dunes, or woods. They are considered the best bicycle paths because they allow you to cycle through nature with no noises other than the songs of birds, while the air you breathe is clean. Such bikeways are almost exclusively recreational paths.

Only a few of Holland's bicycle paths are unpaved—made of sand or dirt, they turn muddy in the rain. All other paths are paved with a variety of materials: asphalt mixed with gravel or with crushed light-colored sea shells that glisten in the sun, concrete tiles, concrete slabs, or bricks arranged upright in herringbone or other patterns.

In addition to the country's network of roadside bicycle paths and bikeways, you may occasionally use a bike lane, marked on the pavement of an urban roadway by a painted white line and a painted white picture of a bicycle.

ANWB Maps for Cyclists

Of the various maps available in Holland for cycling, I prefer the ANWB touristic maps 1 to 14, scale 1 : 100,000. They are loaded with information, uniform for the entire country, and easy to buy in The Netherlands, and at some NBT offices

Some bikeways are soft sandy trails like this one near Nunspeet, in Gelderland province.

41

abroad. These are the maps to which I refer in describing the cycling routes in this book.

The roadside bicycle paths are shown on the ANWB maps as red or black broken lines. The black broken lines represent bicycle paths for cyclists and for people on *brommers* (mopeds), whereas the red broken lines represent bicycle paths only for cyclists. Bikeways, those top-of-the-line bicycle paths, are also shown with black or red broken lines, now without adjacent roads, or as black lines with little teeth. These represent paved touristic bicycle paths, at least 2 meters wide, for cyclists and for people on *brommers*. The Dutch word *toeristisch* as used here by the ANWB means for tourists, and "the most scenic route available."

Bicycle-Specific Signs

Holland is well supplied with signs to help you decide en route which way to go on a bicycle. Blue round shields with a bicycle outlined in white mark roadside bicycle paths and bikeways for cyclists and for people on *brommers*. Black or blue rectangular shields with the word *FIETSPAD* (bicycle path) in white mark roadside bicycle paths or bikeways intended only for cyclists. Sometimes you'll see the words *Dus niet brommen*, reminding moped riders that they are prohibited from the path, as shown in the photo on page 43.

Study the top RH photo on that same page. It shows several ANWB directional signs for cyclists, which are usually red-on-white. The lower directional sign on the right of the post points to an alternate, more scenic route to Blokzijl than the route on the directional sign left of the pole. The sign for the more scenic route is green-on-white instead of red-on-white, and the lettering is in cursive so that color-blind cyclists can notice it.

Below the directional signs is a red-on-white hexagonal sign for a bicycle loop-route (a route that returns you to your starting point). ANWB has signed some 150 loop-routes all over the country with signs of either 30 or 15 centimeter diameter. The routes have names—this one is the Weerribben route—and go via scenic roadside bicycle paths, bikeways, and quiet (scenic) rural roads. ANWB will gradually replace the red-on-white hexagonal bicycle route signs with green-on-white ones. Other organizations also mark loop-routes with signs in different formats.

Signs direct cyclists how to reach a certain point (top left); what options there are; where an ANWB bike route goes (hexagonal sign, top right); whether noisy mopeds are allowed (below —here they are not)

Bringing Your Own Bicycle

If you fly to Holland from overseas you can probably bring your own bicycle on the plane as a piece of luggage for free. This means that you have to go through the hassle of boxing it and, once in Holland, have to worry constantly about the bicycle's safety. There are bicycle thieves in Holland, and your bicycle is probably a good one. If it's a lightweight one, it may not even be very suitable for Holland's paved and tiled bicycle paths, which are often uneven because the Dutch soil sags, for sandy woodland trails where gnarled tree roots stick out, or for old asphalt roads turned into bikeways but full of potholes. For such (infrequent) terrain a mountain bike would be fine but many Dutch view it with suspicion: "When improperly used, the mountain bike, or ATB, is bad for the environment."

Bicycle Rental

Unless your trip through Holland is part of a cycling tour including other European countries, why not *rent* a bicycle in Holland? Bicycle rental shops abound that rent out standard Dutch bicycles. These are no-nonsense vehicles with two wheels, a handlebar, a saddle, lights, a bell, a luggage carrier, and a *terugtraprem*, a back-pedalling or coaster brake. These cycles have no gears and you sit up straight to ride them. If you prefer a bicycle with a little more pizzaz, ask for a similar model with 3 gears and handbrakes—now usually drum brakes which are considered safer than caliper brakes. To date, these bicycles are not as easy to rent as the standard models are; many rental places don't carry three-speeds at all while others sell them early in September when vacation season is over, and don't receive their new supply until May. In areas with some hills (Drenthe, eastern Overijssel, Gelderland, Limburg) and on the Wadden Isles, three-speeds with handbrakes are usually in abundance, however, and there seems to be a trend to make these bikes more readily available everywhere.

In Appendix B you'll find a list of rental shops, arranged by province, that rent out three-speeds with handbrakes.

These are either shops where I obtained a bicycle for my own cycling trips or shops that responded positively to a mailing I did from California in 1990. There are, however, many more places that rent those sometimes elusive three-speeds, in case they are important to you. Inquire locally for addresses.

When you are in Holland, reserve any bicycle at least a day or two ahead. Phoning the shop brings better results than writing a letter, unless you deal with one of the few large establishments that have a secretary and maybe even a brochure in English. Such places may also rent out racing bicycles, mountain bikes, and tandems. (Several of the smaller shops may also have at least one tandem, with or without gears, kept

Some "bikeways," like this one in Overijssel, are no more than the tracks left by farmers cycling through their fields.

in stock for locals who want to take a visually handicapped or otherwise impaired person on a bicycle ride.)

Most rental bikes come with a *snelbinder*, an elastic strap that hooks onto the rear wheel axle and fits over the luggage carrier. You may be able to rent side panniers.

Until recently, almost all bicycle rental shops required a hefty deposit—100 or 200 guilders in *Randstad* cities, 50 elsewhere. More and more shops will now waive the deposit and accept a travelers check or Euro-check instead, to be returned to you when you bring the bicycle back. Most places ask for identification, so bring your passport.

Bicycle Security

Rental bicycles always have a padlock with a key to lock the rear wheel. Sometimes a chain lock is also provided. You should always lock your parked bicycle and, if possible, keep an eye on it, particularly when it carries packed panniers. For example, if you stop at a restaurant, lean your bicycle against a window and take a table behind that window. If possible, park your bicycle inside a garden or shed, or in the guarded bicycle parking called *fietsenstalling* that you will find next to many railway stations.

Bicycles on the Train

To cycle from point A to point B but not back to A, you can in many instances use the train. Buy tickets for your bicycle and yourself at the ticket window; the price for the bicycle in 1990 was either 10 guilders or 7.50 guilders depending on the distance to be traveled. To reach the platform your train leaves from, you may have to go up and down stairs if there is no elevator, or you can't find it. Push your bicycle, perhaps heavy with personal gear in the panniers, up a steep *loopgoot*, a slope of concrete or wood at the side of the stairway. When the train arrives, you have to lift your bicycle—with the panniers removed, if you follow the NS rules—into the freight wagon marked with a blue-and-white bicycle pictogram, and secure, if you wish, the bicycle with string or bungie cords you brought with you so it won't fall over as the train rides. You can sit next to your bicycle on a folding seat or walk to a passenger compartment and sit more comfortably there. You may not board a train with your bicycle before 9:00 on weekdays. This procedure can be a big bother and apparently the Netherlands Board of Tourism agrees. It wrote in its 1990 *Cycling in Holland* brochure, "You can always transport your bikes by train, but be advised it isn't easy .... If there is no room for your bicycle, you have to wait for the next train ..."

Rental panniers are usually of brown canvas, and big enough to hold clothing for a week's trip. The Garster mill is in Nigteveght, in Utrecht province.

Bike and Car

Another way to move about with a bicycle is in a rental car that has a bicycle rack on the back. You can then drive to any point in Holland you fancy, unload your bicycle(s), and pedal away. However, when I made inquiries in 1990 at some of the larger car rental companies, I couldn't find one that rented out cars with a bicycle rack in the back. I was told that the kind of rack the Dutch use requires a *trekhaak*, a trailer hitch to which the rack is attached, and that rental cars don't come with a *trekhaak*.

Since then I have found the owner of a bicycle rental shop who, as part of his service, can make arrangements for you to rent a car with a two-bicycle rear-end rack mounted on a *trekhaak*. (Another one of his services is delivery of a rented bicycle to Schiphol airport or anywhere else in Holland for a modest handling charge.) You'll find his name on the list in Appendix B under North Holland—Nieuwe Niedorp. Other bicycle rental shops have also begun to offer such bicycle delivery service. Car rental companies will, no doubt, eventually offer cars that can accommodate a bicycle rack.

Bicycle Clothing

The 4 million Dutch who use their no-nonsense bikes for transportation every day wear the same clothing on the bike as they do for school, work, shopping, and other mundane routines. Many of the women cycle in skirts (the top half of the rear wheel and the chain are encased in plastic so a skirt can't catch in the spokes or the chain).

When these Dutch cyclists go out for a recreational spin, they often wear the same kind of clothes. You won't look out of place on a Dutch standard bicycle when you wear what you like, except perhaps if you cycle in flashy cycling pants that hug the body and shimmer in the sun.

Always carry a rainsuit. In Holland, ANWB sells them, as do most bike and sporting goods shops. You can buy the kind that keeps you dry in a downpour but doesn't breathe, so you get all wet inside, or the kind that breathes but may not keep you dry in a downpour, at least not if it lasts a while. The latter kind, imported from Scandinavia or the United States, cost more than the non-breathers. Better not to wear a rain poncho, which may blow up in the wind. Sometimes Dutch bicycle shops sell one-size-fits-all reusable plastic rain booties to pull over your shoes in a downpour.

Helmets

Very few Dutch cyclists ever wear helmets for recreational cycling and if you wear yours, you will stand out as a foreign tourist. Dutch children, who are not among the politest in the

Some bikeways are firm and surfaced with crushed seashells, like this one along the Weert loop-route in North Brabant.

world, may laugh at you or ask you in Dutch whether you've had an operation on your head. If you believe in the wisdom of using a helmet, however, wear one. Some Americans I know wore their helmets for the first few days of cycling in Holland, then stopped wearing them, not because they minded being the laughing stock of unmannered schoolchildren, but because they did not feel threatened by automobiles as they did at home. Dutch drivers are used to cyclists since most of them are cyclists themselves sometimes.

Other Cycling Accessories

Consider a sheepskin or other soft padded cover for a triangular saddle if you worry about saddle sores, even if this item is frowned upon by many cyclists as being an affectation. Be sure to take it off the saddle every time you leave your bicycle unattended. A curvimeter is handy to calculate distances. Use one that has a scale on it of 1 : 100,000 if you are going to use ANWB maps and pack a highlighter to mark bicycle routes projected or completed.

You may like to bring a tiny rearview mirror to wear on your helmet or cap to alert yourself to racers hurtling by noiselessly (ignoring the Dutch law that requires the bell) or other traffic, particularly when you cycle on the road. Such mirrors are not known in Holland and make good conversation pieces. Practical for displaying your map while you ride are two clothespins to clip the folded-out map to the wires of your gearshift that loop near your handlebar (not handy when there is a lot of wind). A plastic bag keeps such a map dry.

Route Documentation

In addition to maps that show where the roadside bicycle paths and bikeways are, so that you can chart your own bicycle route, an enormous number of pamphlets, booklets, and books published by all kinds of organizations deal with specific bicycle routes. These publications give you detailed route instructions, sketch maps or map sections, and some or no description of sights. Almost always the text is in Dutch.

If you read the language, inquire about the *Dwarsstap* series, favorites of many Dutch cyclists because each set in this series, also known as *Fietsen in ...,* comes with 1 : 50,000 scale topographical maps. Also popular among the Dutch is the ANWB *Fietsgids* series. Seventeen booklets, each with 20 loop-routes, describe routes and sights, and show each route superimposed on a section of the appropriate ANWB tourist map. Some of the *Fietsgids* routes are also signed with the hexagonal loop-route signs so you can cycle such a loop-route without the *Fietsgids*, but you may like to see on a map where the hexagonal shields are going to lead you. Of course sometimes a sign has been removed, although ANWB tries to remedy the problem quickly, and then you will wish you had a *Fietsgids* to verify the route. On the other hand, this guidebook is one more thing to buy, one more thing to carry around, and you may

At many highway intersections, cyclists have to press a button to change the light.

prefer just to rely on the signs. If you have an ANWB tourist map, you can mark your route as you go so you have a record for later on.

Bicycle Routes in This Book

Since very little route information is available in English, I tell you at the end of chapters 3 through 14 about 20 routes I recently cycled, at least one in every province of Holland. Sometimes I rode with Dutch friends and took their advice. Sometimes I cycled alone and created my own route, looking at the ANWB touristic map for bikeways, roadside bicycle paths, and the thin yellow lines of secondary roads. Several times I followed ANWB or other route signs part of the way.

The routes are listed in the Table of Contents and average 40 kilometers in length. That's a two- or three-hour ride if you keep going, or up to a full day's excursion if you stop for sights along the way.

I strongly recommend that you use the pertinent ANWB map as well, if only to enable you to shorten or lengthen a route, or vary it. You may be ready for a village with a café as I lead you past pastures with cows.

The hotels I mention as possible starting points for the routes are all *fietsvriendelijk*, bicycle-friendly. They welcome cyclists, provide overnight storage for your bicycle, may have local bicycle route information, and may also rent or loan you a bicycle. If a hotel is not your kind, alternate choices are usually available, or you can start your loop-route somewhere else as long as a bicycle rental place is nearby. All the hotels I mention also cater to noncyclists who make up the bulk of the guests. You will find addresses of the hotels in Appendix A and addresses of bicycle rental places I used in Appendix B.

The choice of these 20 bicycle routes is my own, and is only a sample of the hundreds of loop-route possibilities in Holland. If you meet a Dutch cyclist who recommends another route, maybe even rides with you, you may well wind up with a route you like better than the one I suggested.

Part II

Touring
the Provinces

Route map legend

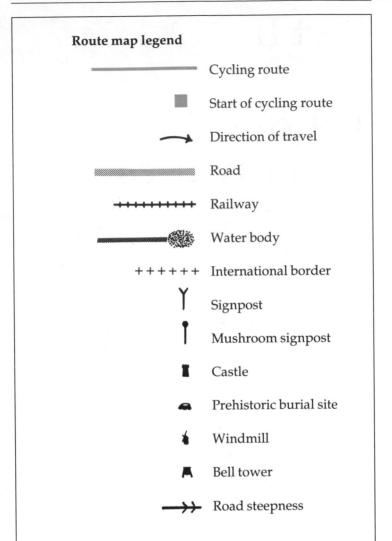

———	Cycling route
■	Start of cycling route
➤	Direction of travel
▧▧▧	Road
++++++++	Railway
▬▬▬✸	Water body
+ + + + + +	International border
Y	Signpost
╎	Mushroom signpost
▮	Castle
▰	Prehistoric burial site
↟	Windmill
♠	Bell tower
→»	Road steepness

Note:

The route maps that accompany the loop-route descriptions in chapters 3–14 are intended for general guidance only. It is recommended to use them in conjunction with the appropriate ANWB 1 : 100,000 scale maps listed in the text.

CHAPTER 3

Drenthe: Bikeway Province

"Drenthe verwent je," Drenthe spoils you, advertises a current tourist brochure. In the first half of the 20th century few people would have thought of Drenthe, in the northeast section of the country, bordering Germany, as a place to go and let themselves be spoiled. At that time, it was still a backwater of The Netherlands, sparsely populated by tenant farmers struggling to grow produce on meager,

sandy soil and by workers toiling in the peat bogs. With long-handled spades, often standing knee-deep in water, they dug up the "brown gold," the peat that brought riches to the

"Hunebedden," prehistoric burial chambers, once covered with sod, are characteristic for Drenthe. This one is in Borger.

individuals or corporations exploiting the bogs—but only miserable wages to the peat diggers.

Then came the discovery of natural gas and oil in Drenthe, and tourism. Not having moat-girded castles, historic towns, imposing ancient cathedrals, or spectacular museums to attract tourists as elsewhere in Holland, people of Drenthe stressed what they did have. That is the tranquillity in its woodsy areas, on its heather-covered moors and, in its small villages with, yes, old churches, small rustic ones made of brick. Drenthe also has scores of small hotels, often family-run and the kind where you are greeted by name and the dining room waiter remembers you're on a low-sodium diet. Best of all, Drenthe has bikeways wending through its appealing landscapes—more bikeways per square kilometer than any other province in the country.

I first heard about Drenthe in third or fourth grade. Drenthe has something unique in The Netherlands, *hunebedden*, ancient burial chambers. We learned they were not built by Huns, although men of science in the 17th century thought so and gave them the misleading name that means "bed of the Huns." In fact, the chambers were built around 2,000 B.C.

When I went to Drenthe 40 years later, I found the *hunebedden* not to be the awesome monuments I had expected, something on the order of the huge prehistoric circle of stones in England's Stonehenge. The largest *hunebed* at Borger, its 47 big stones neatly arranged in an oval, is only 20 meters long, 3.5 meters wide, and 1.8 meters high. Nevertheless, facts relating to the big stones are impressive. Some weigh as much as 15 tons (15,000 kilograms). Diluvial ice must have pushed the stones from Scandinavia all the way to Drenthe, but how did those early men move the boulders towards the burial site and place the heavy cover stones on the uprights of the walls?

The *hunebed* builders are referred to as Funnel Beaker people, because of the shape of pots found in their tombs. Motifs of ears of wheat on the pots suggest that the Funnel Beaker folk were farmers, while beads made of amber or jet suggest they traded, since neither is native to Drenthe soil; did the amber come from Denmark, the jet from England? You can view some of these artifacts in 't Flint'nhoes, a small museum in Borger, or in the Drents Museum in Assen, the provincial capital. All 54 *hunebedden* in Drenthe are marked with symbols on ANWB tourist maps no. 3 and 4. (Before you buy no. 3 make sure you need it: it covers mostly the province of Groningen.) VVV's in Drenthe have literature about the *hunebedden* in English.

In recent years, I have gone to Drenthe with my grandsons and visited the Noorder Dierenpark zoo in Emmen. Here we walked through a hot and humid greenhouse where 1,500 butterflies flutter around among tropical vegetation. Not far east of Emmen, in Barger-Compascuum, near the German border, is the Nationaal Veenpark (*veen* is the Dutch word for peat or bog). You can walk in a 170-hectare (420-acre) park and see a replica of a peat worker's village and an authentic peat terrain. Sometimes a man demonstrates how turf was cut by hand. This park is closed in winter.

Also of interest are the flocks of Drenthe sheep, kept to eat undesirable growth off the heather-covered heaths. In former days sheep were kept for wool and manure until imported

"Klokkestoel," bell tower (see page 64). This one was photographed in Friesland, where most of them are located.

wool became cheaper and chemicals fertilized the fields. Drenthe VVV's have a list of locations where you can find the 9 or so *schaapskudden* (flocks of sheep) that remain, with names and telephone numbers of the *scheper* (shepherd). A good place to see a flock is at a *schaapskooi*, sheep pen (always near a road), when the shepherd, dog, and sheep leave in the morning or return in the afternoon.

As does every province in Holland, Drenthe has numerous museums. Two, very different from each other, are south of Assen. The Museum van Papierknipkunst in Westerbork is a small museum with paper cutting art from around the world; samples go back to the early 18th century. It's sometimes possible to sit for a paper cutting of your face in profile. In Hooghalen is the Memorial Center of the Westerbork concentration camp where Dutch Jews like Anne Frank and her family were herded together before being sent in trains to the death camps. "So this was the deportation camp Westerbork on a Drenthe heath where the week had only 6 days: from Tuesday afternoon to Monday morning. Tuesday afternoon we counted who were left and with those we created something that resembled life. That life continued to Monday morning when the long row of cattle wagons arrived on the rails next to the camp waiting for its weekly load of doomed Jews," wrote Clara Asscher-Pinkhof in *De danseres zonder benen*, Dancer Without Legs.

At the time of writing, Drenthe offered 559 kilometers of roadside bicycle paths and 555 kilometers of bikeways. Of the bikeways, 367 kilometers were two-meter wide, mostly asphalted paths, and 188 kilometers were dirt trails. Using many of these roadside bicycle paths and bikeways as well as quiet rural roads, the provincial VVV of Drenthe has planned 18 bicycle loop-routes, averaging 40 kilometers, and published them in individual pamphlets that cost f 1,50 each. (The Dutch, and most other Europeans, use the comma as the decimal point.) Several of these VVV routes are also in the ANWB *Fietsgids Drenthe*. By 1991 ANWB had signed 8 of the 20 routes with its hexagonal bicycle loop-route signs. Six of these are obstacle-free and marked as being accessible to wheelchair

Onion-steepled St. Nicholas church in Dwingeloo. (Photo courtesy VVV Drenthe)

users, either self-propelled, motorized, or pushed. So far Drenthe is the only province with such facilities.

As starting points for the 2 routes I cycled in Drenthe, I chose Drenthe's capital Assen (pop. 50,000) and Dwingeloo (pop. 3,750).

Assen, 2 hours by train northeast of Amsterdam, is a lively town with several *bruin cafés*, brown cafés—the places without music where the local citizenry meet for a drink and a talk. I stayed at the Hotel de Jonge which has a large area of sidewalk tables and, inside, a large bar with gleaming brass trim. In the adjacent restaurant you can order snacks from the *kleine kaart*, small menu. The hotel's restaurant, Cahors, serves French specialties in a room whose walls are covered with murals of naked nymphs cavorting in a meadow and other whimsical scenes. The hotel is used a lot by businesspeople, many of them foreign. Assen is the headquarters of NAM, *Nederlandse Aardolie Maatschappij* (Netherlands Petroleum Company), a combination of Shell Oil and Exxon that exploits Drenthe's natural gas and oil.

Dwingeloo, a 40-minute bus ride southwest from the NS station in Assen or northeast from the city of Meppel, is a typical Drenthe *brink* village. Its central green, the *brink*, is planted with venerable oak trees, and the people of Dwingeloo will tell you that their *brink* is the most striking in Drenthe. The front windows of little shops and the often stylish fronts of old houses face the green, where people meet to sit down together in a café or, when weather permits, on a terrace outside.

Just off the *brink* is the St. Nicholas church dating back to the 14th century with an "onion" at the steeple, the kind you see in Austria and thereabouts, but rarely in Holland. Opposite this church is Hotel Wesseling where I stayed. This hotel is popular with Dutch from other provinces who come off-season for rest and relaxation, some returning every year. In the past, country hotels in Holland served country-style, hearty Dutch food, but now many serve foreign cuisine, either exclusively or mixed in with Dutch fare. At the Wesseling I ate a very non-Dutch exquisite cod filet steamed with vegetables and herbs in aluminum foil.

Stroomdal Route from Assen (about 48 km)

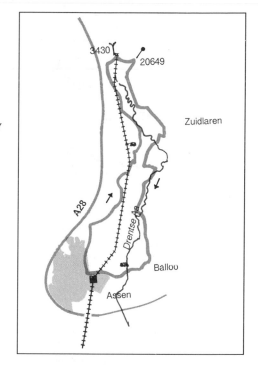

Stroomdal means stream valley and refers to the Drentse Aa (A or Aa is a name for river used in some parts of the country in geographical names).

Additional route information: ANWB Tourist maps nos. 3 and 4. VVV pamphlet *Drenthe Route* 2ab.

Bicycle rental: At NS station.

Starting point: ***Hotel de Jonge, Assen.

Route notes: I cycled this route in late May, and few other cyclists were about. The route includes long stretches of bikeways, mostly asphalted, two meters wide. The country roads were quiet. Towards the top of the loop was an old road turned into a bikeway. To see car traffic in the far distance on the major A28 freeway while peacefully cycling through meadows skirting this bikeway gave a great sense of freedom.

At mushroom 23505 you can make a side trip to a small *hunebed*, 11 stones, in Gasterse *duinen* (sand dunes).

The restaurant near the bridge over the Drentse Aa, which looked lovely with white tables and chairs on a lawn sloping down to the river, was still closed at 12:30 p.m. The Drentse Aa is a gentle brook that flows slowly past clusters of trees, branches dropping into water, as ducks and other waterfowl glide by. Not the Rhine or the Mississippi!

In 1660, the Reverend J. Picardt drew this scene showing how he imagined prehistoric settlers of Drenthe built their tombs. (Illustration courtesy VVV Drenthe)

For lunch, I had a sandwich of wholesome Drents farmer's bread at 't Schepershoes, meaning shepherd's house, off the minute *brink* of Balloo. (Abbreviation *'t* is a contraction of *het*, the Dutch definite neuter article.) Ask at the inn where on Balloër Veld (pink on ANWB tourist map) the shepherd and flock may be.

Posthuis Route from Dwingeloo (about 36 km)

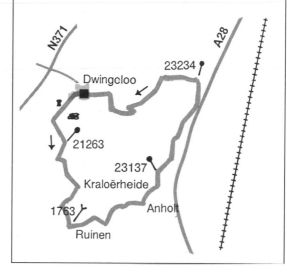

This route is named for a postal coach stop in Anholt where the coach from Groningen changed horses on its way south. The restored inn, now named 't Olde Post-huus, again serves refreshments.

Additional route information: ANWB Tourist map no. 4. VVV pamphlet *Drenthe Route 11*.

Bicycle rental: A.J. Reiber, Dwingeloo, a few doors from the hotel.

Starting point: ***Hotel Wesseling, Dwingeloo.

Route notes: More cyclists were on the bikeways than had been the previous day when I rode the Stroomdal route. Bikeways fan out from Dwingeloo in all directions. Reiber shop can give bicycle renters an English-language booklet, the size of a passport, with 16 routes to choose from (there are no maps in the booklet but you could chart an indicated route on your ANWB map). In summer, the *brink* is chockful of Dutch and German automobiles and cyclists who rent bicycles or bring their own, so if your idea of bliss is cycling nearly alone, visit Dwingeloo off-season. The VVV route pamphlet shows a photo of a flock of sheep on Kraloër Heide (heath, pink on map) and of a mother holding up a small child to a ram, but the sheep are now behind an electric fence. A notice reads *"Pas op, schrikdraad"* (beware, electric fence). The heath now belongs to a large conservation organization, and you are not allowed to walk outside the paths. In this preserve are benches to sit on while looking at little ponds covered with water lilies in pink blooms. You'll see lots of juniper trees.

Another route out of Dwingeloo you might like to cycle is the 46-kilometer Drentse Wold route signed by the ANWB and mapped in its *Fietsgids Drenthe*, mostly along bikeways marked on the map by "teethed" lines. Make a detour to Wapserveen to see a *klokkestoel*, which is a wooden tower with a bell next to a church built when people couldn't afford a real bell tower. As with the *hunebed*, each *klokkestoel* in Holland is marked with a symbol on the ANWB tourist maps.

In Vledder is the small museum Miramar (Spanish for "view of the sea"), where the docents speak English and you can learn about the spare teeth of sharks and the shells of sea snails. Also in Vledder is a 15th-century church with a tower roof in the shape of a saddle.

For a change of locale, consider the popular 49-kilometer Drenthe Route 5, Hunebedroute, published by the Provincial VVV. ANWB includes a similar route in the *Fietsgids Drenthe*, one of the as yet unmarked Drenthe routes. You can stay in the ***Hotel Bieze in Borger which, like the Hotel Wesseling, is an establishment where Dutch from the crowded West like to return to for the chance to get away from it all.

CHAPTER 4

Flevoland: Manmade Province

Some travelers find the province of Flevoland fascinating, while others consider it dull. Indeed, the pancake-flat open landscape tends to be monotonous: roads are straight, fields reach as far as the eye can see in geometric patterns, and farmhouses stand an equal distance apart. The houses all look alike as well: the Dutch government agency that built them was

Northeast Polder from the air is a study in straight lines and square corners. (Photo courtesy KLM Luchtfotografie)

65

able to save some guilders by using the same kind of materials and design for each house and barn. Villages and cities lack the charm and patina of long-established communities elsewhere in The Netherlands and that's precisely what's fascinating about Flevoland. The villages are new, as new as the land they are built on: in the 1930's the whole of Flevoland was still under the water of the Zuiderzee.

For centuries this inland sea had been a menace, flooding surrounding lands when heavy winds blew. Then Dutch water experts executed Dr. Cornelis Lely's 1891 plan, building a 32-kilometer (19-mile) dam to close off and tame the troublesome sea. This dam transformed the sea into the freshwater IJsselmeer (Lake IJssel), and prevented further salination of Dutch soil.

After the dam was built, the water experts reclaimed 3 big pieces of land by building *ringdijken*, encircling dikes, in the lake's water and pumping the inside water out, leaving sections of land called *polders*. (The average depth of the Zuiderzee was 4 meters.) The Noordoostpolder (Northeast Polder) was the first to "fall dry." Ten years later, in 1952, the first settlers moved into the brand-new city of Emmeloord. The Eastern Flevoland polder fell dry in 1957, and in 1967 people began moving into the brand-new city of Lelystad, which is named for the father of the Zuiderzee works. The last to fall dry was the Southern Flevoland polder in 1968. The first residents, many of them workers in the crowded Rim City, moved into brand-new Almere in 1978. In 1986 these 3 polders became Holland's twelfth province, Flevoland, roughly 160,000 hectares (about 350,000 acres or 550 square miles) conjured up out of the waters of the Zuiderzee.

To have a good map for all of Flevoland you will need 3 ANWB tourist maps: the northern part with Emmeloord is on no. 2 with the province of Friesland; the western part including Almere is on no. 5 with part of Rim City; the central part is on no. 7 with Lelystad and the Veluwe, part of the province of Gelderland.

Lelystad is a good point to start a day trip of Flevoland by car or bicycle, and is a 40-minute train ride northeast from Amsterdam. The city (pop. 60,000 with growth potential to

150,000) is a fine example of an entire city sensibly built according to one master plan. Motorized traffic and pedestrians/cyclists move almost everywhere on separate tracks. Downtown, for example, people drive cars at ground level, but ride their bicycles and walk on balustraded ramps a level above. Elsewhere cyclists and pedestrians use bikeways, footpaths, and overpasses made especially for them. On the few occasions that tracks meet there are traffic lights.

In residential parts of Lelystad affordable one-family homes with small gardens, as well as houses adapted for the handicapped, are clustered in named *wijken* (neighborhoods). Streets don't have names: street signs only indicate the house numbers. Most homes are arranged around playgrounds for children and paved planted areas for their elders to walk, sit on a bench, and meet each other. Streets have sharp bends and humps to slow down trafic and end in parking areas between the homes. You can see such residential planning elsewhere in Holland, marked by blue shields displaying the white outline of a house above the word *WOONERF*, literally living yard.

There is much to see in the vicinity of Lelystad. The polder planners created woods and nature reserves (green on your ANWB map) for mushrooms and lichen to grow, for deer,

The still bare new land is spruced up in places by "landart," here on the Ketelmeer dike.

foxes, ermine, and pheasants to find shelter, for birds to settle down and nest, and, of course, for humans to enjoy. Some of the "woods" still look like tree farms, but the trees will be thinned out and, with more light, underbrush will grow.

Of particular interest southwest of Lelystad is a nature reserve that was not planned. This area of lakes, marshes, and reeds left after the draining of the polder was earmarked for industry with the expectation that the area would be covered by growth by the time the developers arrived. But the grey geese ate the expected growth during their spring and fall migrations between Scandinavia and Spain, the lakes and marshes began attracting other migrating birds, and some birds stayed permanently. Two hundred different kinds of birds had visited or settled in the marsh, so the plans for an industry terrain were torn up. The Oostvaardersplassen became a national nature monument and a wetland of international importance (*plas* is a Dutch word for lake).

To protect the wildlife, part of the reserve is closed to the public, but you can walk a trail to an *observatiepost*, a lookout marked on the ANWB map. Or you can get out of your car or off your bicycle on the Oostvaardersdijk and watch all kinds of birds flying, sitting, wading, swimming, and hopping on or near this ringdike. If bird-watching is one of your hobbies, you'll love the Ooostvaardersplassen.

In a 500-hectare nature park, also marked on your map (look for the intersection of A6 and N302 highways south of Lelystad), roam hoofed animals that include antlered reindeer, humped wisents of the bison family, and Przewalski horses. These 1.30-meter tall horses, with a coffee-with-cream color and short upright dark-brown manes, are named for a Russian colonel who rediscovered them in Mongolia at the end of the 19th century. The breed is believed to date back to prehistoric times and to have always lived in the wilds until the last 10 or so generations. When it appeared that the horses were to become extinct, they were kept and bred in zoos. An international program is now under way to re-educate and properly breed the horses so they can be let loose in the wilds again. As part of the conditioning process they are taken care of in semi-reserves like the Natuurpark Lelystad. Pick up a park map and explanation in English at the entrance to the park, and hope that the animals will be visible. The park organization recommends binoculars.

If your interest goes to agriculture, ask the VVV Flevoland in Lelystad how to make an appointment with a local farmer. Some are members of the Nautilus Cooperative and concentrate on what the Dutch call biological-dynamic farming, which emphasizes quality and respect for the environment. In due time this cooperative may have an information center. At Bronsweg 50 is the Terra Nova shop where you can buy organically grown tomatoes and fresh bread (made with grains grown in the new polder) for a picnic in what not so long ago was the Zuiderzee.

You almost pass the Bronsweg on your way from the center of Lelystad to the shore of IJsselmeer and the Nieuw Land Information Center, marked on your ANWB map. Here you can learn about the making of the IJsselmeer polders, although you may have to wait for a presentation in English until one in another language is finished.

Next to New Land you'll probably be able to see work in progress on the reconstruction of a wooden seafaring ship of

Statue to honor the stone setters who laid the basalt blocks of the enclosing dam by hand. (Photo Madelyn van Rijckevorsel)

the 17th century. When I was at the site in 1991, a team of mostly volunteers was working on a replica of the *Batavia*, a ship nearly 60 meters long that left Amsterdam in 1628 to fetch spices in the Far East but foundered off the Australian coast. The replica was scheduled to be finished in 1992 or 1993 complete with 3 masts (the tallest is 53 meters), rigging, sails, and sculptured wood decorations including a life-size lion on the bowsprit, all made in the 17th-century manner. Plans are for her to sail around the world for the promotion of Holland while the replica of another 17th-century ship would be started in Lelystad.

If time permits, continue your drive or cycle clockwise along Lake IJssel. On your left you will pass the approach to a dike with a road on it that veers off into the water, seemingly to nowhere. This is the Markerwaard dike, which slashes 17 kilometers through IJsselmeer to Enkhuizen in the province of North Holland. The dike was built in anticipation of yet another IJsselmeer polder, and the road atop it was opened in 1976. But before land reclamation was started, the Dutch began reconsidering the use of the proposed land, slated for agriculture. The matter is still being debated, as the ANWB map shows: Markerwaard *(in studie)*.

In the Museum voor Scheepsarcheologie (Museum for Maritime Archeology), less than 20 kilometers east of here in Ketelhaven, are wrecks of ships uncovered during the reclaiming of the land. Since the Zuiderzee was never more than 4 meters deep, the ships that foundered here between the 14th and 20th century were mostly those used for inland navigation and much smaller than, for example, the seafaring *Batavia*.

One of the wrecks in the museum is still in a humidity-proof tent to dry out as part of her preservation process. Around 1700 she transported live fish in her hold, which you can see through a window in the tent. With the ships sank clothes and household inventories: shoes, crockery, pewter and brass objects, and 6 eggs found in a 17th-century wreck are all on display here.

If you continue driving or cycling along the edge of the polder, you can see an innovation in polder making, the *randmeren*, or border lakes. No such lake was built between the

Noordoostpolder and the old land; as a result the old land began drying out. The border lakes of the 2 Flevoland polders keep the adjacent old land moist, at the same time providing space for sailing, windsurfing, fishing, swimming, and sunbathing. The Dutch deposited enormous amounts of sand along the edges of the border lakes to create their sandy beaches.

You could also reverse your travel direction and cross the Ketelbrug into the Noordoostpolder, (Northeast polder), the oldest of the three. It offers the same geometric landscapes as the more recent polders do, but the trees along the roads are taller and the woods offer more variety.

Two unusual attractions in the Noordoostpolder are the *Orchideeënhoeve* (orchid farm), between Luttelgeest and Bant, and the wind turbine park near Urk. The former is open all year to show off some of its 100 species of orchids that bloom there. In the wind turbine park on the IJsselmeer dike stand 25 sleek white poles with 3 blades at the top that whirl in the wind and create enough energy to generate electricity for 3,000 homes. Currently the Dutch produce only 16 megawatts of this environmentally sound energy in Urk and a few other places,

Wreck of 17th-century merchant vessel that sank in the Zuiderzee. (Photo courtesy Scheepsarcheologiemuseum)

but in 1989 the government drew up a plan to generate 1,000 megawatts by the year 2000.

The ANWB shows the location of these new-style windmills on their maps with a symbol and the word *windturbinepark*. (If you are cycling and wonder what *Fietsers bij gedogen* means, as printed on ANWB map no. 2 near the wind turbines, it means that cyclists are permitted, but at their own risk—you are on a private road.)

When the village of Urk was an island in the Zuiderzee, most Urker men fished for a living. Now that Urk has become part of the new land, the Urkers still fish but have to go through the locks in the Enclosing Dam to throw their nets in the North Sea. They bring back plaice, cod, herring, and other saltwater fish, making Urk a good place to eat fresh fish. Restaurants are closed on Sundays.

In talking about Flevoland the Dutch often talk about "the polders" (as in "I'm driving through the polders"). Although a large part of The Netherlands is made up of polders, none are as large as those of Flevoland. If your budget permits, a quick way to see the polders is from a small three-passenger plane. Flights of 15 minutes or more leave from Lelystad airport.

If you are cycling, it is easy to decide what you want to see and chart your own route with an ANWB map. All bikeways are marked on the map. The secondary roads (marked in yellow) are lightly traveled. Be aware that distances between coffee shops, restrooms, and such may be longer than you are used to in the old land. Wind is always a possibility out in the polder.

The route I cycled touches on all the sights near Lelystad I mentioned above and overlaps part of ANWB's Nieuw Land Route, signed with the hexagonal ANWB bicycle route signs.

Lelystad Circle Route (about 45 km)

Additional route information: ANWB tourist map no. 7. Route partially overlaps ANWB's signed Nieuw Land route.

Bicycle rental and starting point: At NS railway station. If you need a hotel, try the

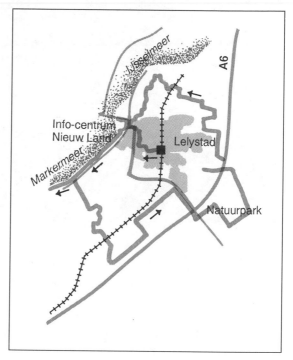

****Hotel Lelystad, opposite the VVV in Lelystad. It has 218 beds and caters mostly to businesspeople and to busloads of tourists, foreign and Dutch, who come to see the new polders.

Route notes: If you get lost in the Lelystad *wijken*, town quarters, on your way to the Nieuw Land information center, head for a tall radio and television tower, marked on a city map as *PTT straalzender*. It's close to the information center.

For rides in the Noordoostpolder go to Emmeloord (take the train to Lelystad or Kampen, regional bus from there). You can rent a bicycle in Emmeloord, although when I inquired, only standard bicycles with coaster brakes, without gears, were available. You'll need ANWB map no. 2.

Once the railway line extension from Lelystad to Emmeloord is finished, you're likely to find a bicycle rental facility at the new NS station. From Emmeloord, you could ride the

Hothouse filled with moth orchids (phalaenopsis) is open to the public in the Northeast Polder. (Photo courtesy Orchideeënhoeve)

20-odd km to the Urk wind turbine park that is a modest beginning of things to come all over Holland. The EGD, the electricity generating board of Groningen and Drenthe, for example, will have 80 wind turbines in operation by the mid-1990's. They will be manufactured by a San Francisco-based firm (with more than 15,000 units in operation, California is way ahead of windswept Holland when it comes to using wind power to generate electricity).

CHAPTER 5

Friesland: Home of "Us Mem"

You'll find her on a traffic circle on the Harlingersingel in Leeuwarden, capital of Friesland, a well-proportioned cow cast in bronze. She stands there on a pedestal to honor all the cows and their milk and byproducts in the province and all its international cattle-breeding transactions, pillars of Friesland's economy. She's called *"Us Mem,"* Friesian for "Our Mother."

Skûtsjes, typical Friesian sailing boats, line up before a race. (Photo courtesy VVV Friesland)

Friesian rather than Dutch is spoken at home by most of the 500,000 to 600,000 Friesians here. Now recognized as a language, not just as another dialect in the collection of roughly 25 dialects still extant in The Netherlands, Friesian is taught, and sometimes used for teaching other subjects, in the province's schools. In recent years Friesian has also been used at times alongside Dutch in official provincial documents, in special columns in Friesland newspapers, in churches, and for plays performed by amateur and professional theater groups.

As a visitor you won't notice much of this movement to preserve the Friesian heritage, but it explains the bilingual place name signs you'll see along the roads, e.g. Ljouwert and, underneath, Leeuwarden; the first is Friesian, the second Dutch. The Dutch name is the one you will find on maps. (The ANWB tourist map for Friesland is no. 2.) You'll also see Friesian flags flying, or pictured on cookie tins and other tourist souvenirs: 7 red water-lily leaves over 3 white diagonal stripes that alternate with 3 similar stripes in blue.

Friesland is a land of water and much of it is in the lakes of the southwest. Should you be in Friesland in summer, inquire at a VVV when and where the next *Skûtsjesilen* will be held, a race between the characteristic Friesian sailing vessels called *skûtsjes*. Once used for carrying freight, 14 of these flat-bottomed sailing boats with retractable leeboards are now owned mainly by towns or corporations, and only used for competitive sailing. Tall masts heightened, big sails enlarged for the race, the clumsy-looking *skûtsjes* manned by crews of ambitious Friesians pick up considerable speed if the wind is blowing. Crowds of spectators along the lakeshore cheer for the winning *skûtsje*, or jeer when one capsizes, big flat bottom up in the water.

South of a lake called Slotermeer lies Sloten, smallest of the 11 medieval *steden* of Friesland. *Steden* is plural of the Dutch word *stad*, which is defined as "a usually walled place with its own government and jurisdiction ..., separated from and independent of the rural area," but also as "a large urban area." Throughout this book I use "town" for the (still recognizable) medieval Dutch *stad*, and "city" for its sprawling modern counterpart (which probably grew from a medieval town). In later chapters I'll mention other medieval towns you may like to visit. The 11 medieval towns of Friesland are now linked by the skating tour that I discuss later in this chapter.

Sloten, once favorably located on an intersection of waterways and the only road leading north, received town rights in 1250. For a while the town prospered, then knew decline, and never grew beyond what must have been its size in 1250. Fewer than 800 people live in Sloten today. They make a living from a cattle-feed factory, a yacht harbor, and a steady stream of tourists who on a nice day sit down at sidewalk café tables along Sloten's one *stadsgracht*, town canal. The canal is flanked by restored old-time houses with neck gables and step gables, among others, of the sort you also see on the houses along the canals of Amsterdam.

Of the other 10 Friesland towns, small Hindeloopen (pop. 800) on the shores of IJsselmeer may be of interest. The Dutch like it for its little wooden bridges *(bruggetjes)* that arch over its little canals *(grachtjes)*. Like Sloten, Hindeloopen zeroed in on water tourism and has a lively yacht harbor. In the town, shops sell unique wooden wares handpainted with traditional Hindelooper designs: trays, boxes, or ladder-back chairs with a

Workum potter decorating an earthenware bowl.

rush seat. Shops ship worldwide if you have too much luggage to take a Hindeloopen purchase with you on a plane.

North of Hindeloopen is the town of Workum (pop. 4,200), where potters make jugs and bowls and plates of a green or rust colored earthenware decorated with a simple cream colored border. Workshops are open to the public; ask Workum VVV where to go. The Workum ware is inexpensive, at least compared with the elaborately painted majolica ware of the Tichelaar factory in the village of Makkum farther north. The factory and a small museum with a collection of centuries-old Makkum ware can both be visited.

The town of Sneek (pop. 30,000) has a one-of-a-kind water gate left from the days when the town was walled and traffic came in on the water. Bolsward (pop. 10,000) has an ornate red brick town hall from the 17th century, and Franeker (pop. 21,000) has a planetarium that wool comber Eise Eisinga finished building in his home in 1781. Except for a few war-caused interruptions the heavenly bodies have been revolving on his ceiling ever since and are still "on time."

The largest town of the 11 is Leeuwarden. With a population of 85,000 it is now a city, but the canals and bridges of its old center still remind you of the past. The ceramics museum, at Grote Kerkstraat 11, displays pieces from all over the world. Dokkum (pop. 12,500), the farthest north of the 11 towns, also has a well-preserved historic center. Some of the old ramparts have been reconstructed. Two 19th-century windmills stand on an old bastion.

The 11 towns of Friesland are known all over Holland as a group; few non-Friesian Dutch would be able to list them by name. The towns are associated with the *elfstedentocht*, 11-town tour, an ardous 200-km (120-mile) skating marathon that passes through all the towns. This means skating on stretches of uneven ice, hunkering to skate under low bridges, and walking past bridges when the ice underneath is too thin, all of this usually in bitterly cold weather. The first official *elfstedentocht* was in 1909 with 22 participants; the winner completed the course in 13 hours and 20 minutes. Since then the skating tour has been organized any year that ice conditions permitted. In 1986, last tour at the time of writing, 17,000 skaters participated, although only 300 were in it for a race, the others for the satisfaction of having done it. The winner of the race was Evert van Benthem, who had also won in 1985. His time in 1986 was 6 hours and 55 minutes. It is estimated that more than half the population of The Netherlands followed the day-long event live on television, without interruptions for commercials. Of the other half, a great number journeyed to Friesland to see the event close up. "Most sensational tour skater was W. A. van Buren," reported one Dutch newspaper and explained that he was supposed to be incognito but spectators knew he was 18-year-old Crown Prince Willem-Alexander.

Other 11-town races are organized too: on a bicycle, a surfboad, or by foot-propelled scooter. The surfboard marathon is in spring, the one on the scooter on Whit Sunday, and the bicycle tour on what the Dutch call "third Whitsun day," meaning the Tuesday after Whit Monday, a national holiday. The organizers advise that interested cyclists should apply between mid-January and mid-February. Names are drawn and the cutoff point is 15,000. In 1991 an equal number were on the waiting list.

The jet-black Friesian horse is used for harness events, here in a Workum street, more often in parks or rings. (Photo Frans Andringa)

There's more to Friesland than the lakes and the 11 towns. Drive or cycle in the north of Friesland via the secondary roads (yellow lines on ANWB tourist maps) and discover small villages with a church and perhaps part of the village built on a *terp*. This is a mound that the early Friesians piled on the flat land as a refuge for man and beast when the sea waters rose. They did this at least from the 2nd century, when Roman writers recorded it, to the 11th century, after which the building of protective dikes began. VVV's in Friesland can give you a pamphlet on the *Terpen Route*. You will also see the typical Friesian head-neck-trunk farms with enormous sloping roofs that sit like brooding hens in the pasture: the family lives in the head, the cattle in the trunk, and the neck connects the two. Go to the big dike at Friesland's northern edge and see the Wadden Sea, filled with water at high tide, without water at low tide.

In Marssum, near Leeuwarden, is Popta Castle, an impressive home built in the 16th century, with period furniture and a toilet lavishly decorated with blue Delft tiles. Tours are offered several times a day. In Joure, in the southwest, are several clock makers who make true copies of antique pendulum clocks.

For a cycling route in Friesland, I chose one through the Gaasterland region in the southwest: it has some woods, is not absolutely flat (as is typical of most of the rest of Friesland), and includes one of the 11 towns, Sloten. You could add Hindeloopen and Workum if you were to cycle a lot in one day or stay over for another day. You can reach the starting point of Koudum by regional bus from the railroad stations of Heerenveen or Leeuwarden (limited service on weekends).

I stayed for one night in the ***Apartment Hotel Galamadammen, 1 kilometer south of Koudum with a large terrace overlooking a lake. Since then the hotel has expanded with accommodations in the four-star category and its own yacht rental facility. Apartments are still available, in season only by the week.

Gaasterland Route from Koudum (about 50 km)

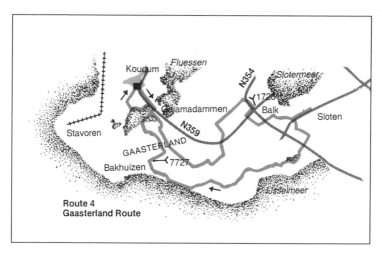

Additional route information: ANWB tourist map no. 2. This route overlaps almost entirely the Gaasterlânpaad (Friesian word) mapped in the ANWB *Fietsgids Friesland*, no. 14, and signed. Watch for the hexagonal route signs.

Bicycle rental: Autobedrijf Kemker, Koudum.

Starting point: ****Hotel Galamadammen.

The Friesian clock, photographed in a Dutch home, strikes the hour and half hour; the weight has to be pulled up twice a day.

81

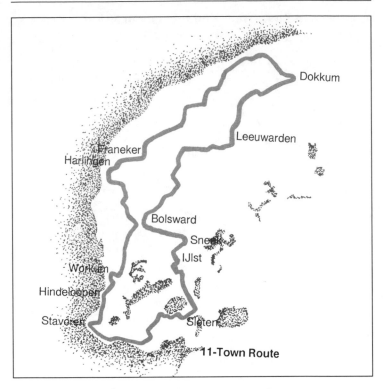

Dokkum

Leeuwarden

Franeker
Harlingen

Bolsward

Sneek

IJlst

Workum

Hindeloopen

Stavoren

Sloten

11-Town Route

Route notes: Balk has a handsome little 17th-century town hall and, going right through the village, a canal lined on both sides with linden trees. I encountered little motor traffic on the "yellow roads," but in season traffic to and from sailing and surfboard areas is likely to be heavy.

Friesland doesn't have many bikeways, the kind that meander off alone, but it does have lots of bicycle paths parallelling the roads and used by locals for going to school or shops or relatives and friends. Bicycles with 3 speeds and handbrakes were not for rent at several places I inquired.

As for an alternate route, if you have several days you could bicycle the 230-kilometer 11-town route signed by the ANWB. Camp along the way, sleep in the country hotels, or stay in private homes in farm country. Ask any VVV in Friesland for a folder of *Bêd & Brochje* (Friesian for Bed and Breakfast).

CHAPTER 6

Gelderland: Big Rivers and a National Park

Gelderland, in the eastern part of the country, is the largest of Holland's 12 provinces. It has 3 distinct regions: the Veluwe (sandy, slightly hilly, woodsy), the Achterhoek (more fertile, also slightly hilly, woodsy), and the Gelderland river area (flat, open polderland). For detailed maps of the respective areas use ANWB tourist maps no. 7, 9, and again 7, plus, if you

In Gelderland's Veluwe region, some sand is allowed to drift, not anchored down with vegetation as is done in the precious coastal dunes.

need the most western tip of the river area, no. 6.

Holland's biggest national park, the 5,500-hectare (13,600-acre) Hoge Veluwe, is in the Veluwe, and this park has an interesting history. Around the time of the First World War, the Dutch business man Anton Kröller and his German wife Hélène Kröller-Müller had a monumental lodge built on Veluwe wasteland. Anton was a hunter and the house, now part of the park, is a stone visualization of the life of St. Hubert, patron saint of hunters. A booklet in English, for sale at the park entrance, explains how the legend of 8th-century Hubert inspired designs of the lodge and the rooms.

Hélène collected art. As the years went by, Anton bought more wasteland to increase his hunting grounds and Hélène bought more art. In the 1930's, Anton and Hélène bequeathed their estate and the art to the Dutch state, on the condition that the art would remain in the park. Hélène's fabulous collection—too large to display at one time—includes 278 Van Gogh paintings, pastels, and sketches, Mondrians, Picassos, Seurats, and earlier masters. Outside the Kröller-Müller museum, in a 16-hectare sculpture garden, are works by Henry Moore and other contemporary sculptors. Half a million visitors tour the sculpture garden, museum, and park each year.

To see this once private domain, drive from either of the 2 north entrances, Hoenderloo or Otterlo, along a road that traverses the park to the south entrance at Schaarsbergen or vice versa. You can also cycle on a 40-kilometer network of asphalted bikeways, away from automobile traffic, or walk along a network of footpaths, some of them marked with the small color-bearing posts of signed walks. Buy a map at the entrance. In the park you may walk outside the footpaths, something forbidden in many public places in Holland. The only restrictions in Hoge Veluwe are areas posted *Rustgebied voor het grofwild*, resting area for big game. During the rutting season of the deer, from mid-September to mid-October, the *wildbaan*, the reserve where the big game lives and mates, can only be crossed via the motor road, either by car or bicycle.

The big game of the Hoge Veluwe consists of the native wild boar and deer that Anton Kröller hunted. The moufflons, wild sheep with impressive curled horns, were imported from

Corsica and Sardinia to replace the domestic sheep that grazed on the Veluwe moors before the Kröller-Müllers purchased the grounds, relocating the few poor sheep farmers outside their estate. At observation posts you may be able to see the wild animals close up; evenings are the best time. The park closes at sunset, which in summer can be as late as 10 o'clock.

If you come to the park in a car and would like to cycle, 500 white bicycles stand in racks near the visitors' center. Made in a style to fit bikers from age 6 upward, these sturdy bicycles with coaster brakes are for visitors to use inside the park. Saddles and handlebars are adjustable. Once you have selected your white bike and are off on it, do not leave it unattended. Some visitors seem to be under the impression that they may pick up a white bike anywhere in the park. If you plan to leave your bicycle temporarily parked while you go for a hike, bring a lock for the bike.

Hélène Kröller-Müller would have approved of the *kinder-bos*, children's forest, planted in 1985 during the park's 50th anniversary year. All 700-odd parents of babies born that year in The Netherlands on the park's birthday, April 26, were asked by mail to give the park permission to plant a tree for the new child. Planted were 560 oaks of the *quercus robur*

In the Hoge Veluwe park, this truck regularly makes the rounds to retrieve the (free) white bikes that are abandoned by some of the visitors.

variety, called *zomereik,* summer oak, in Dutch, that can live for up to 500 years. Each child received a certificate with the tree's number and may come any time with a parent to see how his or her tree has grown.

South of the park lies the city of Arnhem and on its outskirts the Openluchtmuseum, Open Air Museum. Here you can stroll among windmills, several types of farms, a small church dating from 1672, an old school, and other curiosa of times long past. In Oosterbeek, just west of Arnhem, is the Airborne Museum, commemorating the battle of Arnhem in 1944 during the Second World War. An audio-visual presentation is in English.

North of the Hoge Veluwe, near the city of Apeldoorn lies the Palace Het Loo (pronounce "low"). The family of the present Dutch Queen Beatrix, the House of Orange, built this palace, a smaller copy of the Versailles palace near Paris, in the 17th century. The last Orange to live at Het Loo was Queen Wilhelmina upon her abdication in 1948. After her death the palace was restored to its original condition and turned into a national museum, filled with opulent and ornate furniture, vases, tapestries, velvet wall coverings, murals, painted and sculpted ceilings, crystal chandeliers, gold-trimmed columns, and oil paintings of various Oranges—alone, in family groups, or in battle scenes. You may walk through the rooms on your own if you don't want to join a guided tour. Printed material in English is available. All 3 museums mentioned are on the ANWB map.

At the northern edge of the Veluwe on the Veluwemeer, one of the lakes dividing Gelderland and Flevoland, lies the old town of Harderwijk (town rights in 1231). Once it was a flourishing port on the Zuiderzee. As a member of the German Hanseatic League, Harderwijk traded wool from England, cloth from Belgium (made with English wool), sea salt from France, wine from Germany, wood, herring, and furs from Scandinavia and the Baltic states—all transported over the seas and waterways of northwestern Europe. Harderwijk's walls were recently restored, as were some of the old buildings and facades. The facades may not be altered, but alterations made behind the facades are usually allowed, provided a permit is in hand. The town has a modern *dolfinarium*, a place where dolphins show their tricks.

At a stall along the quay of Harderwijk you can eat eel caught in the IJsselmeer and smoked locally. Eel is also served in Harderwijk restaurants, smoked, fresh and poached, or fresh and fried, with or without rich sauces.

East from here you will reach the river IJssel, beyond which lies the province of Overijssel. Turn south to remain in Gelderland and enter the Achterhoek region, which extends east from the IJssel to the German border. Achterhoek means back corner. Dutch from the flatland enjoy the landscape of Achterhoek: wooded areas alternating with fields, not separated by watery ditches as in the polderland, but by hedges and trees.

Through this landscape flow little rivers down modest hills with enough force to activate waterwheel mills. Some of the mills have been here for centuries, fell into disuse, and now have been restored as national monuments. All working waterwheel mills in the Achterhoek are marked with the appropriate symbol on the ANWB tourist map no. 8

Like many of the working windmills of The Netherlands, the waterwheel mills operate only on certain days at certain times. Achterhoek VVV's can tell you the schedule. The miller

Part of the Deelense Zand in the Hoge Veluwe park is covered with purple moor grass (molinia coerulea).

moves a lever or a handle in the mill house to release the water from the adjacent stream that turns the waterwheel and works the mill. The Dutch windmill, on the other hand, may remain idle in spite of what the tourist literature says. It depends on the wind.

The Achterhoek has its share of medieval towns. Two are on the IJssel and, like Harderwijk, profited from the Hanseatic trade. In Zutphen (town rights in 1190), you'll find built onto the St. Walburgis church the Librije, one of the very rare well-preserved "chain libraries" in western Europe. You can look at some of the original books, chained to the original 16th-century pulpits, that were placed there by the library founders to counteract the Reformation. In Doesburg (town rights in 1237), is an unusual blue stone near the splendid Gothic town hall. The city fathers would place a cage with the town's prostitute on the stone so the populace could taunt her for her sins.

The smallest town in Gelderland (also on the IJssel) is Bronkhorst (town rights in 1482): a few historic houses on both sides of a short winding street you can drive or cycle through in a few minutes. De Gouden Leeuw (The Golden Lion) restaurant serves anything from coffee to a banquet in an authentic historic setting, as does Het Wapen van Bronkhorst. A cheese farm, Het Hoge Huis (The Tall House), also several centuries old, sells *boerenkaas*, farmers' cheese. Such cheese is sold all over The Netherlands in shops or at farms you'll pass as you tour the countryside. The milk of the cheese comes from the farm's own cattle that graze on pastures fertilized as much as possible in the natural manner. The cheese remains unpasteurized to preserve the milk's aroma and taste.

A car ferry crosses the IJssel to Brummen and you may want to include it in your itinerary just to cross one of Holland's rivers in this manner. Even more interesting are the ferries for pedestrians and cyclists only, the *voetveren*, which will be discussed in chapter 12.

The Achterhoek is known for its many castles. The ANWB has marked them on its tourist map no. 9. The second symbol is for a castle open to the public, which usually means that you can see the inside only on a guided tour. Inquire before you pay the entrance fee what kind of tour it is: Does the guide have the time and the training to tell you in English what she just told the other visitors in Dutch? What is there to see inside? You can view most castles in Holland from the outside for free. The surrounding gardens are likely to be well kept and pleasing to the eye.

The Gelderland river area stretches between Arnhem and Nijmegen on the east and Gorinchem on the west, and is closed in by the river Rhine (also called Neder Rijn and Lek) in the north and the river Meuse in the south. The river Waal slices from east to west through the center. With the exception of some hills near Nijmegen, the river area is absolutely flat and looks very Dutch with dikes lining the rivers to keep the river water off the land. In the rivers are *kribben,* piers made of stones and willow twigs that jut at regular intervals into the water to reduce the river's width and thus protect its shores. On the rivers are barges and *duwboten,* boats pushing a string of tenders. They carry freight to and from Germany, Belgium, and Switzerland. Beyond the rivers are farms, some hugging the non-river side of the dike so that as you drive or cycle on it, you are on a level with the farm roofs.

Low-slung barge on the Rhine near Arnhem makes one wonder what she's transporting.

On ANWB tourist map no. 7 you'll see above the Waal in large capital letters BETUWE. This is "Holland's orchard." The Dutch drive to the Betuwe in spring to see the blossoming apple and pear trees. On a famous Appeldijkje, Little Apple Dike, between Marienwaard and Tricht, heavy "blossom traffic" may have to be led in a one-way loop. Fruit trees are forced to grow low so the fruit is easier to pick. This makes some of the blossom watchers nostalgic for the tall spreading trees of yesteryear.

The river area is a place where you may want to drive or cycle without a set route through the farm country and past the cows. Check your map for bridges or ferries, since you may have to detour to cross a river, and stick to the roads marked yellow on the ANWB map.

There are also old towns in the Betuwe. Take tiny Buren, so small, it's said, that on a windy day the keeper of one town gate called to the keeper of another gate, "Please close your gate, I feel a draft." (The Kuypersgate can still be seen.) Buren has a windmill, the Oranje Molen: the town once belonged to

Marta Pan's 1965 floating polyester sculpture ...

the Orange family. Queen Beatrix still has the title of Countess van Buren, along with a host of other titles. It's from this town that members of the Orange family take the Van Buren name they use when traveling incognito, as the Crown Prince did in 1986 when he participated in the *Elfstedentocht*, the 11-town ice skating race in Friesland.

Not far from Buren on the south shore of the Waal is one of Holland's most famous castles, Loevestein, complete with moat, drawbridge, turrets, and shooting holes in heavy brick walls. The castle was built in the 14th century as a fortified mansion, but turned into a state prison in the 17th. Dutch schoolchildren learn that during a 12-year truce in the Eighty-Year War against Spain (1568-1648) the Orange prince then in power incarcerated his political opponent, the Dutch jurist and humanist Hugo Grotius, in Loevestein. Grotius escaped hidden in a blanket chest. Only 5 such chests now exist, including one in Amsterdam's Rijksmuseum and one in Loevestein, but no one knows which chest, if any, is the original one. You will probably have to join a guided tour to see the inside of the

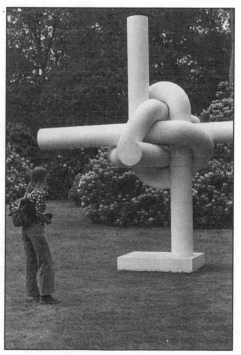

... and Tajiri Shinkichi's 1969 polyester knot no. 4 are among the works of art on display in the Hoge Veluwe's sculpture garden.

castle. The guide may only tell her story in Dutch, but a guidebook in English is available. You may walk alone on a footpath over the ramparts.

For a hotel in the Veluwe as base for a cycling loop, I chose Arnhem's ****Rijnhotel. Take a bus or taxi from the NS station. The hotel is built right on the Rhine, so you can watch the river traffic pass by as you sit on the balcony of a riverside room or at a window table of the restaurant. (The restaurant offers several vegetarian entrées. The one I tried was very good and cost less than an entrée with meat or fish.)

Arnhem is a big city (pop. over 100,000) and has many hotel accommodations from which to choose. With a fast Intercity train you can get there in about an hour from Amsterdam.

A hotel in the same category as Rijnhotel, but in the country, is ****Hotel Buunderkamp in Wolfheze, surrounded by woods and not far from the south entrance of the Hoge Veluwe. The hotel provides bicycles with coaster- or handbrakes and has bicycle route suggestions in English. To reach the hotel by public transportation, take a train to Wolfheze and call a

This farmhouse snuggles safely up against the dike in Alblasserwaard, but if the dike has to be raised, the house will have to go.

taxi to drive you the 2.5 kilometers to the hotel. (Taxi number is posted in telephone booth.) Not far from the Buunderkamp is Doorwerth Castle (a real one with moat and drawbridge), which houses a small hunting museum and a deluxe restaurant. The maître d' may suggest a surprise dinner of 3, 4, or 5 courses for which the chef will decide the menu, coming to your table to announce before each course what will be served next. Make reservations ahead of time.

In the Achterhoek I stayed in **Hotel Bakker in Vorden, one of those long-established, well-run small country hotels you'll find on many of Holland's backroads. Vorden is on a railroad line.

On the following pages, you will find 3 bicycle routes, one for each of Gelderland's 3 regions: Veluwe, Achterhoek, river area. For the last route, the Betuwe route, I took the train to and from Tiel from my base in Amsterdam, so I don't have a river area hotel to suggest for you.

Let me add a note here about what constitutes a castle in the eyes of the Dutch tourist industry. You may expect a medieval fortified dwelling with moat, drawbridge, sturdy walls, and towers from which to observe, and shoot at, intruders. But the ANWB and VVV's designate as castles almost all large dwellings, including the rural mansions called *staten* in Friesland, *borgen* in Groningen, and *havezaten* in Drenthe. If all these are included, there are about 300 "castles" in the Netherlands.

Hoge Veluwe Route from Arnhem (about 40 km)

Additional route information: ANWB tourist map no. 7.

Bicycle rental: Wim Roelofs Tweewielers. This shop is a few blocks from the NS station. First pick up a city map at the VVV on square outside station. You can also ask there how to ride from the bicycle shop to your hotel.

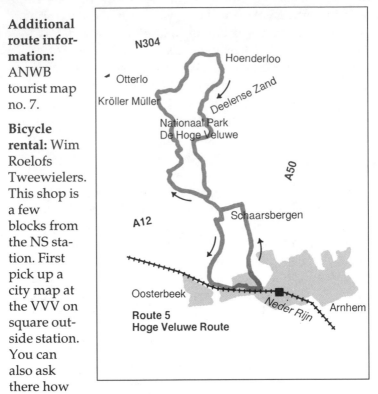

Starting point: ****Rijnhotel in Arnhem.

Route notes: This route will take you to the Schaarsbergen (south) entrance of the Hoge Veluwe National Park. You'll need a map to see how to get there. You have to go through some heavily traveled areas, so be careful.

Buy a park map at the entrance. You probably won't see many other cyclists about until you are close to the restaurant, the information center, and the white bicycle storage racks. The Kröller-Müller Museum and the sculpture garden are close to the restaurant. All over the park ANWB mushrooms show you the way.

Eight Castles Route from Vorden (about 30 km)

Additional route information: ANWB map no. 9. The hotel has a VVV folder showing the route. An inlay translates the Dutch text.

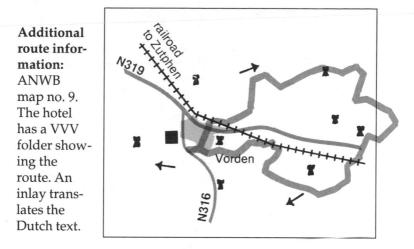

Bicycle rental and starting point: **Hotel Bakker.

Route notes: You cycle past a number of dignified mansions set in stately parks. In spring, rhododendrons bloom in towering masses of purple and pink. Here and there you ride under canopies of great old oaks and beeches. This is an easy tour to cycle: flat and, thanks to the many trees, protected. You may hear cuckoos calling.

Betuwe Route from Tiel (about 55 km)

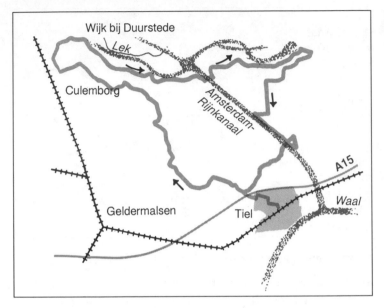

Additional route information: ANWB maps 6 and 7. ANWB *Fietsgids Gelders Rivierengebied*, route no. 4. This route is signed with the hexagonal Betuwe route shields.

Bicycle rental: NS station. Three-speeds with handbrakes may not be available.

Starting point: NS station Tiel.

Route notes: You pass the small town of Buren. From the northern part of the route you have fine views over the river Lek. You could detour to the town of Wijk-bij-Duurstede described in the Utrecht chapter, crossing the Lek by ferry. The Betuwe route passes over the Amsterdam-Rijnkanaal twice. The bridges have bicycle paths—pause on a bridge to watch the river traffic sail underneath.

CHAPTER 7

Groningen: Tidal Flats and Romanesque Churches

At the top of Holland lie the 2 Groningens, the city and the province. Groningers will tell you that you shouldn't miss Groningen city (pop. 186,000), which they consider "one of the 3 real cities of The Netherlands" (Amsterdam and Maastricht being the other two). A real city is explained as being "full of culture and *gezelligheid,*" that hard-to-translate Dutch word mean-

Bourtange fortress, restored to its 16th-century glory, lies in the Groningen polderland. (Photo Aerophoto Eelde)

97

ing something like coziness and ambiance. Groningen city is less than 3 hours from Amsterdam by Intercity train.

Groningers will also be happy to point out the touristic merits of Groningen province, topped by its fine collection of old churches. Indeed, if you are interested in the way artisans guided by monks built churches here 600 or 700 years ago, in frescoes (or seccoes) of the time, in pulpits and pipe organs of a later but still long-ago time, then Groningen province is for you. More than 100 old churches—many in tiny villages—lie scattered over the polderland. VVV Groningen has printed information in English on the subject, and ANWB tourist map no. 3 shows you with a symbol where the churches are. About half are still used for worship.

The oldest churches date back to the 12th and 13th centuries and were often built on a *wierde*, a mound for refuge in times of flood (in Friesland the mound is called a *terp*). Inside the church, artists painted saints and biblical figures or, more frequently, ornamental designs with watercolors on the moist (or dry) plaster of ceiling and walls. When Protestant re-formers took over the Catholic churches centuries later, they covered the frescoes with whitewash. In the 20th century, restorers removed the whitewash and brought the frescoes back. The intricately sculpted wooden pulpits date from the Protestant era, and organs built by famous organ builders like Arp Schnitger and A. A. Hinsz can be found as well.

If you play the organ, you may want to go to Groningen province the second Saturday in May when De Orgelland Stichting, Organ Land Foundation, organizes its annual Noord-Nederland organ day. For one modest fee you may play for up to 20 minutes on any of the organs of some 40 participating churches. A few are in Friesland or Drenthe. To play a specific organ another day, write to the foundation, in care of the Provincial VVV Groningen at the address in Appendix A.

To visit the inside of any of the old churches you will probably have to fetch a key from the *koster*, church sexton, or from another local person. A notice at the church door advises, usually only in Dutch, where to go. Don't be in a hurry: The keeper of the key may have strolled to his neighbor's house for a cup of coffee or be out tending a cow or a horse. Avoid Sundays.

There is a concentration of old churches north of Appingedam, which is 25 kilometers (15 miles) by car from Groningen city. The churches I found most fascinating are:

Marsum (12th century). No furnishings inside. Church door is usually unlocked.

Bierum (13th century). On melon ceiling (looks like slices of melon) are decorative frescoes. Pulpit was made about 1650.

Krewerd (13th century, tower 15th). Organ was made in 1531 and is still in use for church services or concerts. This church can only be visited upon permission of the Old Groningen Churches Foundation; write them in care of the Groningen VVV, or phone the keepers of the key, Mr. or Mrs. Bos, at the Pastorieweg in Krewerd 05960-22347.

Godlinze (12th century, tower heightened 1554). Has ceiling paintings and a Schnitger organ from 1704.

Small church perched on a mound in Marsum. This saddle-roof church dates from the 12th century.

Zeerijp (14th century, tower 15th). Inside walls are completely covered with the original painted-on bright red bricks, hidden for centuries under whitewash and restored in the 1960's.

After viewing these churches, you can drive or cycle to the Menkemaborg in Uithuizen, or make a separate bicycle trip (see Cycling Information at the end of this chapter). The *borg*, castle, is marked on the ANWB map with the castle-open-to-the-public symbol. You can wander through the furnished rooms of this moat-girded brick mansion without a guide.

Around the villages of Uithuizen and Usquert are large farmhouses that resemble the head-neck-trunk farms of Friesland, with family and cattle all under one big sloping roof. Other houses are villas built by well-known architects who adorned them with Italian-style pilasters. You are in the Gold Coast of Groningen, as locals call it, where some of the richest families of The Netherlands used to live. The wealth of these families came from agriculture on Groningen's fertile polder soil, much of which was added by man. The village of Usquert, for example, once lay on the Wadden Sea. Now it is 5 kilometers inland, separated from the sea by a sea polder.

On your ANWB tourist map you'll see along the Wadden Sea coast brown broken lines and the word *landaanwinning*, land reclamation. Land reclamation through dike building is no longer cost-effective, so the sea will be allowed to make its alluvial deposits but no dike will be built.

For a look at this Wadden Sea, go by a canal called Noordpolderzijl and climb the steps of the big sea dike recently heightened for safety reasons. If the tide is high you will see the little harbor filled with shrimp boats, nets draped over the masts, and beyond stretches water. Or, if the tide is low, the harbor will be a puddle of mud, without boats, and beyond mudflats as far as you can see.

You may want to try the Dutch sport of *wadlopen*. The word means walking on the *wad*, mud or tidal flat. You must engage a trained guide or join a scheduled guided group tour. From Pieterburen in Groningen or from Wierum in Friesland you cross the *wad* to one of the Wadden islands and walk or take a ferry boat back. The walk takes several hours. You can also make a shorter and less strenuous *zwerftocht*, a roaming tour, and stay close to the Friesland or Groningen coast.

Be prepared for a muddy start as you slip and slither in the black gooey mud of the alluvial deposits. Soon you pass through the mud to walk on the firm rippled sand of the sea bottom in a world you never walked in before: a world of sea gulls and other birds flying around you, of little creatures wriggling in the wet sand, of bracing air, of smell of sea, and of an enormous sky. During part of your journey you will not be within sight of any land. Several hours later this whole vast expanse will again be sea. Ask VVV Friesland or Groningen for addresses of *wadlopen* organizations.

The Groningers call the northern part of Groningen (between Zoutkamp and Roodeschool) Het Hogeland, The High Country, because of subtle differences in altitude you are not likely to notice when you travel about. The name does not appear on the ANWB tourist map.

The southeast part of the province, called Westerwolde and shown on ANWB tourist map no. 4, does not seem to be overrun by tourists. You will pass the same kind of isolated farms and large fields (many with wheat or potatoes) as in the Hogeland. "When the potatoes bloom white or light purple,

"Wadlopen" entails walking on the sandy bottom of the Wadden Sea, and sometimes wading through deep gulleys. (Photo Nusi Dekker)

late May or June, they are as striking as the bulb fields," said a Groninger. But there are also woodsy areas and little brooks here. Close to the German border lies Bourtange, a carefully restored 17th-century fortification with star-shaped ramparts, a moat into which bastions project, and V-shaped ravelins outside the moat on which cannons stood to protect the works between the bastions.

I stayed one night at the ***Hotel Homan in nearby Sellingen, a pleasant hotel fronted by a café terrace with white chairs and tables, as nearly every village hotel or country inn in Holland provides. On a sunny day these terraces fill up with both locals and visitors. You can reach Sellingen by regional bus from the NS stations of either Emmen to the south or Winschoten to the north.

The other hotel I stayed in in Groningen province was the *****Familiehotel in Paterswolde. I picked it for its location in the country but only 7 kilometers from the NS station in Groningen city (the regional bus stops in front of the hotel), as well as being near Drenthe with its many bikeways. It is *fietsvriendelijk*, bicycle-friendly: bicycles on loan from the hotel and bicycle route suggestions (in English) at the reception desk.

A few kilometers from the hotel is Eelde's *bloemenveiling*, one of Holland's 8 flower auctions. The auction starts at 6:30 a.m. and from a visitor gallery you can watch the buyers sitting on a steeply tiered tribune. Below, carts with flowers or plants are trundled by the auctioneer as 2 sales go on simultaneously. Two clocks with enormous dials indicate growers' code numbers, the quality of the items as determined earlier by the inspectors, the quantity of items left, and, of course, the price, which the auctioneer calls out as the dial moves downward. The clock stops when a buyer on the tribune pushes a button.

The Eelde auction is much smaller and not as impressive as the one in Aalsmeer near Amsterdam, but you feel the same tension as the buyers sit with fingers on the button in front of them, ready to press it before someone else does, and the flowers on the carts going by the auctioneer are just as beautiful as those in Aalsmeer. You receive a folder in English when you pay the entrance fee at the gate and may be able to join a

Lakenvelder cows are a rare breed appearing all black with a white sheet tied around their trunk, seen here in Metbroek Park near Vlagtwedde, in Groningen province. (Photo Henk van Lenning)

guided tour of the auction halls. Ask the Eelde VVV or Groningen VVV for details.

In planning a trip through Groningen province by train or regional bus, bear in mind that their routes all radiate from Groningen city, so you may have to return there before going somewhere else. You can reach any outpost by public transportation but it may take a while.

Old Churches Route from Appingedam (about 30 km)

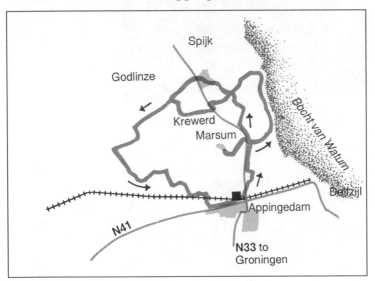

Additional route information: ANWB tourist map no. 3.

Bicycle rental and starting point: Appingedam NS station.

Hotel: *****Familiehotel in Paterswolde or any hotel in Appingedam or on a connecting railroad line.

Route notes: Tailor this route to the number of churches you wish to visit. If you have time you may want to stop off first at the huge Nicolai church in Appingedam to see the interesting floral frescoes on the ceiling and a Hinsz organ. You cycle mostly on winding rural roads without much traffic and without trees. You'll probably love this wide open farm country when the sun is shining and no fierce wind blows. The countryside tends to take on a bleak and somber air under dark overcast skies. Along the Eems coast you'll see the words *Fietsers bij gedogen* again (meaning "cyclists are permitted, but at their own risk"). The dike road here is not surfaced and tends to be muddy after rains.

You can make a separate cycling trip out of Uithuizermeeden. Bicycle rental is available at Rijwielverhuur Idema, 200 meters from NS station. Take the following 50-kilometer route: head

Appingedam's Grote Nicolai church was started around 1225. The organ dates from 1774. (Photo Jan Hovinga)

for the Wadden Sea coast, going first west, then right (north) at ANWB pole 9217. At the sea dike turn west again as far as Visafslag (fish auction), south along Noordpolderzijl, then follow the yellow roads to include Usquert, Warffum, Rottum, Middelstum, Huizinge, Westeremden, Garsthuizen, Zandeweer, Menkemaborg, and back to Uithuizermeeden.

Bourtange Route from Sellingen (about 35 km)

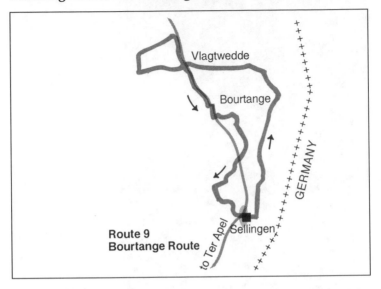

Additional route information: ANWB map no. 4 (Drenthe map).

Bicycle rental and starting point: ***Hotel Homan in Sellingen. It can arrange for bicycles.

Route notes: Between Vlagtwedde and Onstwedde in the Metbroek woods (on the map) you may see an unusual Dutch type of cow, the Lakenvelder. They are so called because of a white "sheet" (*laken* in Dutch) they seem to wear tied over the middle of their totally black rump. The little park belongs to the Natuurmonumenten organization, and the Lakenvelder is used as a "natural mowing machine" of meadows in spring and summer.

CHAPTER 8

Limburg: Province with the Highest Hills

In a country as flat as The Netherlands, ridges of 1,000 feet seem spectacular or, at least, noteworthy. You'll find these heights in the south of Limburg on ANWB tourist map no. 14, near Maastricht (pop. 125,000), a 2½-hour Intercity train ride southeast from Amsterdam.

Maastricht is old. More than 2,000 years ago the Romans founded it at Mosae Trajectum, ford of the Meuse. In the Bonnefantenmuseum for art and antiquities you can see

Not far from Maastricht is Heerlen, with ruins of Roman bathhouses. (Photo courtesy Thermenmuseum)

local archeological finds from Roman times. This museum will move in a few years to the new Ceramique Park development.

After the Romans left, Maastricht was for centuries the seat of Christian bishops. The first one, Servatius, died probably in 384. Some of his remains are preserved in a sumptuous 12th-century golden shrine on view at the treasury of the St. Servatius church.

In the Middle Ages, Maastricht was surrounded by walls, several of which still stand in city parks. Also from the Middle Ages date a number of monumental churches, including St. Servatius and, a few blocks away, the Onze Lieve Vrouwe Basiliek, basilica of Our Beloved Lady. Both are in the Romanesque style but, with their large size and elaborate interior ornamentations of sculpted stone or wood, they are different from the sober, small Romanesque churches in Groningen province.

In the 19th century Maastricht became the capital of a new Dutch province called Limburg and has now grown from a sleepy backwater town to a city that attracts international conventions, commerce, and tourism. Promotional brochures stress the Burgundian atmosphere of the city and the Burgundian spirit of the Limburgers which, to the Dutch, means exuberant, knowing how to enjoy the good things of life. The word goes back to the 14th-century court of the duke of Burgundy at which the arts and flamboyant behavior flourished. You may not find the Limburgers you meet flamboyant, but you may well find them more easygoing and outgoing than the Dutch up north, or as the Dutch often say "above the rivers" (the Rhine and the Meuse that slice the country horizontally in two).

Located close to Germany and Belgium, Maastricht is a good base for day trips across the borders. You can drive or take a train to Cologne to see the marvelous Gothic cathedral, completely restored from bomb damage sustained during the Second World War, or stand on a bridge over the Rhine and watch the water traffic go by. Or you could go to Liège, which has a great old town center, and eat a big rich Belgian waffle.

The countryside around Maastricht is hilly, with some highways and many winding country roads that go steeply up and down. On your ANWB tourist map no. 14, you'll note the > or < signs on the roads to indicate whether they go up or down, as you move from left to right. Some of the backroads here are what the locals call *holle wegen* (hollow roads), meaning hollowed out by centuries of farm cart traffic and by water rushing down. Often lined by hedges that obscure the side views, the hollow roads treat you to sudden wide panoramas when you reach the top.

On your rural rambles you'll see farmhouses that differ from those elsewhere in Holland. Dutch provinces, and even some regions, built, and often still build, farms in their own traditional style. The typical Limburg farm is built of red brick in a rectangular shape with a large, probably cobbled, courtyard in the center, just as the Romans built their *villae*, farmsteads. You enter the courtyard through tall arched double doors usually painted dark green. Also typical for Limburg are two- or three-story *vakwerk* houses. Outside walls expose a framework of dark beams; the spaces in between are filled with a mix of braided twigs and loam and then covered with whitewash.

Along the country roads you may see statues of Christ on the cross or tiny chapels with a statue of the Virgin Mary and

"Vakwerk," timber-frame buildings, like this hotel in Mechelen, are characteristic of Limburg. (Illustration courtesy Hotel de Plei)

perhaps a jar of fresh flowers in front. Limburg has long been predominantly Catholic, whereas the provinces in the North have been predominantly Protestant.

On a hill near Margraten (east of Maastricht) lies a piece of land that The Netherlands has granted in perpetuity to the United States as a final resting place for 8,000 American soldiers killed nearby in the Second World War. Older Limburgers, upon meeting an American visitor, may express their gratitude to America for liberating Limburg in 1944 (the North was not liberated until May 1945).

Two large murals at the Margraten cemetery explain with maps and text in English the Allied operations in the West European theaters. For a panoramic view of the cemetery and the lovely hills where such fierce fighting took place, ask the custodian (at right when you go up the steps to the pond) for a key to the tower of the monument. You have to climb 149 steps to the observation platform.

Scattered among the hills are various castles, some turned into hotels. The hotels I stayed in are ***Castle Wittem in Wittem (train to Wijlre, taxi to castle) and ***Castle Erenstein in Kerkrade (train to Kerkrade, taxi to hotel). At the Erenstein, the restaurant is in the castle and the hotel is in a remodeled old Limburg-style farmstead. A few kilometers away is a similar remodeled farm, the ***Winselerhof (same owner as Erenstein). The room prices in Erenstein and Winselerhof are quite reasonable, but breakfast is not included.

You may enjoy the Thermenmuseum, an unusual museum in Heerlen built over the ruins of *thermae* (Roman public bathhouses) uncovered there in 1940. The history of the Roman baths, which were a center of leisure and recreation, may inspire you to join other tourists in the warm pure waters of Thermae 2000, a modern spa built on a hill in Valkenburg. For a fixed fee you can use all the pools, jacuzzis, and exercise rooms for a number of hours, but the sauna costs extra. Note that men's and women's facilities in the sauna are not separate. Drive or take a train to Valkenburg and go by taxi from there or walk the steep hill. The Dutch Railroads sometimes offer a day outing that includes a bus from the NS station in Maastricht to Thermae 2000 (more about such day outings with the railways in chapter 18).

South Limburg, a popular vacation destination for the Dutch, has a multitude of hotels in all categories. In Maastricht, I stayed at the ****Hotel de l'Empereur, which recently underwent a giant remodeling and expansion, and nearby the smaller ***Hotel Bergère. (In Limburg, French is used not only by some restaurants for menus, as it is also done up north, but occasionally for names of hotels as well.)

On a cycling trip once, I had a cup of tea in the ***Hotel-Café Wippelsdaal in Groot Welsden near Margraten. This would be a good choice if you are traveling with children since it is combined with a farm. The terrace has a wide view over the hills. You can reach the hotel via regional bus fom NS station in Maastricht. Bicycles are for rent in Margraten. Note that the castle hotels described above have the same number of stars as this country inn. The castle hotels are formal, with *à la carte* meals at deluxe restaurant prices, while this country inn is informal with *table d'hôte* (little or no choice) meals for pension guests. There's obviously diversity within one classification, reflected in the room prices.

South Limburg's scenery is different from that of the rest of the country. The hills are crisscrossed by footpaths and there are plenty of benches on which to rest and enjoy the scenery.

The long, narrow province of Limburg follows the course of the sinuous Meuse and, next to it, the near-straight and more navigable Juliana canal. If you're driving up or down the province on the A2 freeway, you can take the Born exit and drive a short distance west to the double locks in the Juliana canal as indicated on ANWB tourist map no. 13. You'll probably see some large commercial barges slowly sink or rise in the lock chamber as the water therein goes down or up.

Farther north is a one-of-a-kind place, the white town of Thorn (pop. 3,000). The houses here are all painted white, many with red geraniums in the windows, and the streets are cobbled, some with colored mosaic patterns. The history of the town is special: around the year 990 an abbey was founded with a convent for women and a monastery for men. The men left, and the convent was converted into a secular convent for ladies from the highest nobility. They spent their lives in luxury, each in a stately house, and were free to marry if so inclined. Their abbess was the princess of the principality of Thorn, with its own coinage, jurisdiction, and legislation. This lasted until the end of the 18th century. Only the abbey church now remains of this extraordinary arrangement, a church mostly white inside with an ornate, gilded baroque altar (it closes at 5 o'clock). There's a fee to go in unless you go for a service. Not far from the church is a recent "Statue to Music" that caused quite a stir because the 2 bronze flautists are naked.

In season, Thorn is a favorite destination for tourist buses, but at the end of the afternoon they're usually gone. In the evening local citizens may be marching in their *harmonie* (brass band). Every Limburg community seems to have one, with men and women dressed in colorful uniforms.

You can reach Thorn by taking the train to Roermond or Weert and then a regional bus which takes half an hour, or take a taxi, particularly when you're several in a group. In the Thorn area are asparagus fields, long strips of molded earth under which most of Holland's white asparagus are grown. The asparagus season is May and June, when many restaurants, especially those in Limburg, offer special asparagus menus. Friends and I enjoyed an all-asparagus menu at the ***Hostellerie La Ville Blanche in Thorn when I last stayed there:

As soon as the asparagus show their heads in fields like this, they'll be harvested. (Photo courtesy VVV Limburg)

Salad of asparagus and sweetbread
Clear asparagus soup
Poached salmon with asparagus in lemon sauce
Asparagus Flamande
Choice of desserts

Limburg doesn't have as many bikeways away from cars as some of the other provinces have, but if you like to pump up a hill for the sheer pleasure of then coasting down, go to South Limburg. Along many roads are roadside bicycle paths, but do be careful cycling around the curves of winding rural roads when hedges obscure your view.

I chose 2 routes starting at places already discussed: the capital of Limburg, Maastricht, and the little whitewashed town of Thorn.

Margraten Route from Maastricht (about 33 km)

Additional route information:
ANWB tourist map no. 14

Bicycle rental: NS station Maastricht

Starting point: Any Maastricht hotel. The 2 I mentioned above are near the NS station.

Route notes: To find your way out of Maastricht, pick up a city map at the VVV in the center of town, a 10-minute walk from the NS station. The first part of the cycle route is on a roadside bicycle path following the Meuse river or a tributary water pool. After Eysden you turn inland and

A dedicated crew cleans the white crosses at the U.S. military cemetery in Margraten

St. Servatius church in Maastricht watches over the Vrijthof at night. During the day, the square is surrounded by crowded terrace cafés. (Photo courtesy VVV Limburg)

the climbs begin. After Bruisterbosch you will see the big white tower of the U.S. military cemetery, but it still takes a while to get to the entrance via a stretch of narrow bumpy roadside bicycle path alongside N278. To return to Maastricht, after crossing the N278, many cyclists opt for the steep "Bemelerberg descent," but it has several blind curves and lots of traffic. Instead, right after 't Rooth make a sharp left turn, past the fence of the marl quarry, down an unpaved road. You may have to walk your bicycle. This road also leads you back to the N278 and Maastricht. You'll be glad for the roadside bicycle paths (wide and paved) along roads leading into Maastricht where big trucks lumber next to you.

Meuse Villages Route from Thorn (about 30 km)

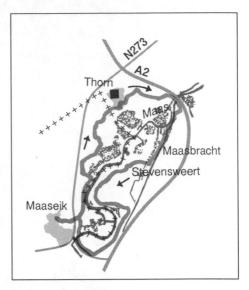

Additional route information: ANWB map no. 13. There is an informative pamphlet about the route available at the Thorn VVV.

Bicycle rental and starting point: ***Hostellerie La Ville Blanche.

Route notes: I chose this route because it passes Maasbracht, an inland port where hundreds of river barges may be moored at one time. Nearby are the impressive triple locks in the Juliana canal. Maaseik, just across the border in Belgium, has a cobbled market square surrounded by very handsome old facades and places to eat the rich Belgian waffles. For part of this route you have to look at the big clunky towers of an electric power plant. Such towers are hard to hide in a flat land.

This route has been signed with hexagonal bicycle route signs by the town district Roermond. Occasionally the route crosses the ANWB Maas Route, so be sure to follow the right signs.

If you'd like to make another foray out of Thorn, consider a 12-kilometer ride to the bicycle bridge over the Meuse. You'll find it by cycling to Wessem, under the A2 to Pol and on to Heel, over double locks in the Linne-Buggenum canal (marked with a symbol on map), and arriving at the Meuse and the bridge. Hostellerie La Ville Blanche has a route description in English for guests.

CHAPTER 9

North Brabant: Van Gogh and an Old Cathedral

"Nothing would seem simple than painting farmers or ragpickers or other laborers, but no subjects are as difficult to paint as those everyday figures," wrote Vincent van Gogh to his brother Theo in July 1885. He was writing from Nuenen in North Brabant, where he lived for 2 years with his parents. Seeing the village where van Gogh painted *The Potato Eaters* is a

These carillon bells hang in a church in Hattem and overlook the Apeldoornskanaal. (Photo Johannes Weiss, courtesy Beiaardmuseum)

good reason to visit North Brabant—another province "below the rivers." Brabant is historically much like Limburg: in the past predominantly Catholic, late in being admitted to the family of Dutch provinces, and once poor but now gaining economic strength through industrialization and increased farming.

You'll find Nuenen on ANWB tourist map no. 11, 5 kilometers east of Eindhoven, home of the electronic giant Philips. Drive or take a regional bus from Eindhoven's train station, or rent a bicycle there. A Van Gogh documentation center in Nuenen covers his 2 years in the village (1883–1885). A brochure in English gives you extracts from Vincent's letters to his brother. About his parents, Vincent writes, "Their reluctance to have me in the house is similar to how they would feel about having a big rough dog in the house. He will come into the living room with wet feet. (...) He will get into everyone's way. He barks loudly." (Letter 346) And when the Catholic priest had forbidden his parishioners to pose as Vincent's models, "The time has come to break out, after all that trouble of finding models. (...) The priest went so far as to promise people money if they did not let themselves be painted." (Letters 433 and 42)

The Center also has information in English about a walk past places related to Vincent's Nuenen sojourn, such as the room where he painted the peasants who ate the potatoes. But you can't see the mangle room in the rectory that his father let him use as a painting studio because another Dutch Reformed minister now lives in the rectory.

East of Nuenen, in the village of Asten, is the Dutch National Carillon Museum, the only such museum in The Netherlands. Drive there, or take a train to Eindhoven and then a regional bus, or rent a bicycle at NS station in Eindhoven (standard bicycles only). It's a 20-kilometer ride to Asten using the bicycle path (black broken line on the map) along Eindhovenskanaal.

Carillons are again popular in Holland; in the 17th century a carillon in a church tower was a status symbol for a Lowlands town. In your travels, you may hear bells from the tower of a church or a city hall being played mechanically or by a live carillonneur. In the museum you can see a carillon keyboard and how the keys connect with wires to the clappers of bells high in a tower. Perhaps someone will be playing a chorale by Bach or a modern piece by the Dutch composer Henk Bading, pounding the keys with the sides of his or her lightly clenched fists.

In the museum's archeology section are examples of the first known bells. They were made in ancient China long before the birth of Christ: small clapperless earthenware or bronze bells hit with a wooden hammer and used to accompany songs. In the swinging bell department are big bronze bells of the Middle Ages that hung in church towers and were used to call people to worship, to tell them of a fire (with the fire bell), or of an official verdict having been proclaimed (with the heavier *banklok*, the proclamation bell). Visitors to the museum may pull the thick rope of one of the centuries-old swinging bells and hear its booming sound.

The church in Nuenen, painted by Vincent van Gogh, still stands. (Photo courtesy Vincent van Gogh Foundation/ Vincent van Gogh Museum, Amsterdam)

North of Eindhoven in the town of Best is Klompenmuseum De Platijn, a museum that displays examples of wooden shoes from many ages and many countries. *Klompen*, wooden shoes, have long been associated with Holland, even though they are not a Dutch invention. Still, the Dutch probably wear more *klompen* for working in the fields or in their gardens than any other people in the world; 3.5 million pairs are made each year. They are made of poplar wood, either by machine or by hand, in 35 *klompenmakerijen*, wooden shoe factories. The manual process is demonstrated in the Bros. Laarhoven *klompenmakerij* next to the museum (which they also operate). The museum may be unique, but you can see *klompenmakers* at work in Rim City and other areas where tourists gather. *Platijn* is the word for a medieval *klomp*, merely a wooden sole kept in place with straps.

Another good reason to visit North Brabant is the splendid Gothic cathedral in the provincial capital of 's Hertogenbosch. The *'s* is a contraction of *des* which is old Dutch for "of the," and the whole name means "woods of the duke" (the medieval duke of Brabant). English speakers, finding the name hard to pronounce, often call the town by its French name Bois-le-Duc. Some Dutch say "Den Bosch" (the "ch" is silent).

The cathedral (started in 1380) was built over the next 200 years, during which time Den Bosch was one of the largest towns of the Low Countries, thriving on trade and small industries. Cloth, leather, shoes, knives, and pins were shipped via waterways all over Western Europe. Be sure to see the "peaman" right above the high portal to the left of the main entrance. He is said to be modeled after one of the supervisors of the cathedral's construction. Not pleased with the pot of cooked peas his wife brought him for his noon meal, he cried "That is no food for a man who earns a copper penny a day!" and kicked the pot away with his feet. You can see the peas rolling out, but you have to look up 11 meters as you stand on the sidewalk.

Not far from the cathedral, the VVV has offices in one of the oldest houses in town, a short walk from the station if you are coming by train.

From Den Bosch it is some 15 kilometers to Heusden, an old town on the Meuse and a textbook example of restoration. Existing buildings have been renovated and buildings and defense structures long since gone have been copied on the basis of old drawings. The result is a little town that looks very much as it did in the 17th century, complete with ramparts built as a star and bastions, moat, and ravelins—just like Bourtange in Groningen province.

A look at ANWB map no. 11 will tell you that Brabant is cut up by highways and freeways, but you will also see the yellow lines of secondary roads, patches of green for woods, and patches of pink for heath and wasteland. (If you go to the very southern part of North Brabant, you'll need map no. 13.) Not all pink or green areas are equally exciting. Much is made, for example, of a new nature monument, De Groote Peel, a former peat area which became famous, or rather infamous, to an older generation of Dutch familiar with the books of Anton Coolen. His book *Peelwerkers*, Workers in the Peel, published in 1930, is a somber, depressing story about ignorance, poverty, hard work in the peat bogs, and little hope for a better life. Interesting to walk on now are *knuppelbruggetjes*, walkways made of logs *(knuppels)* laid like little bridges *(bruggetjes)* next to each other over marshy areas. I found the reserve rather dull; maybe the dreary weather had something to do with it. In eastern North Brabant I like the Strabrechtse heide, which reminded me of the heaths in the Hoge Veluwe National Park, and the Loonse and Drunense Duinen, a future national park called Europe's largest sandbox because of its many sand dunes.

The only hotel in North Brabant at which I stayed as I scouted the bicycle routes below is the small *Hotel Terminus in 's Hertogenbosch, conveniently located near the NS railroad station. Not all the rooms have their own toilet and bath. Locals come here for a drink and a game of billiards at the pool table.

For the second route in Brabant I stayed in ****Hotel Jan van der Croon in Weert, just over the provincial line in Limburg. This hotel is big enough to accommodate busloads of foreign tourists overnight or to feed Dutch groups on a day outing. The hotel serves both Neerlands Dis and Tourist Menus.

Heusden Route from 's Hertogenbosch (about 55 km)

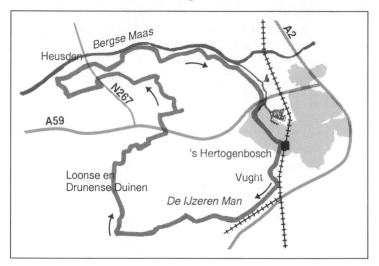

Additional route information: ANWB tourist map no. 11.

Bicycle rental: NS station 's Hertogenbosch.

Starting point: NS station or your hotel.

Route notes: The first 15 kilometers follow the Loonse en Drunense Duinen Route (no. 18 out of ANWB *Fietsgids Westelijk Brabant*) past the suburb Vught and the lake IJzeren Man as far as the restaurant De Rustende Jager. At the restaurant, mushroom 21797, make a right-hand turn (the ANWB sign announces *routeverkorting*, shortcut). Just before Nieuwkuijk is the windmill Emma which sells open-faced sandwiches of *molenbrood*, mill bread.

After Heusden is one of the most memorable sections of all my rides that spring. Pedaling high on the dike on a bikeway for cyclists only (broken red line on map), you have the Meuse (here called Bergse Maas) on your left with very green pastures with cows and red-roofed farms beyond. On your right, below you, are more pastures and cows and farms. Some of the pastures were covered with bright yellow buttercups and dandelions, and you may see a barge gliding down the river. After this tranquil section the route continues back to 's Hertogenbosch along the river on a secondary road where only once in a while a car passes.

The interior of the St. John cathedral in Den Bosch has a serene, stately beauty. (Photo Ernst van Mackelenbergh)

Weert Route from Weert (in Limburg) (about 38 km)

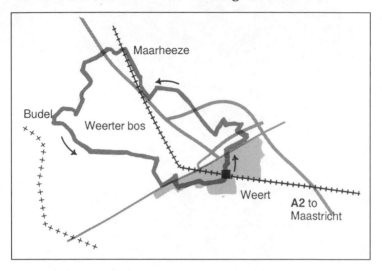

Additional route information: ANWB map no. 13.

Bicycle rental: Jansen's Verhuur at edge of Weert will deliver rental bicycles to any Weert hotel.

Starting point: ****Hotel Jan van der Croon, a few blocks from NS station.

Route notes: This route straddles parts of Limburg and North Brabant. The ride doesn't have any terrific highlights like the ride above, but is a pleasing mixture of windmills, woods, small river valleys, cultivated land, and settlements that include residential sections with red brick villas surrounded by cheerful, colorful, well-kept gardens. In Budel a tree-lined street was so darkened by branches meeting at the top that I felt I was cycling through a dimly lit cathedral. A sign suggested that motorists switch on their lights.

CHAPTER 10

North Holland: Dikes, Windmills, and Polders

"The province Holland is too big in size, population, wealth, and incomes in relation to the other provinces," said representatives of the Dutch people in 1840, and the province was divided into North and South Holland. In South Holland you'll find the international port of Rotterdam and The Hague, where the residence of the Queen,

This farm with a pyramid-shaped roof in the Beemsterpolder is typical of North Holland. (Photo courtesy NBT)

125

the Dutch parliament, and numerous Dutch government offices are. In North Holland you'll find Amsterdam, capital of the nation, and, if you have never been there, a city you may want to visit before heading for the backroads of North Holland. (We do not cover Amsterdam in this guidebook.)

You can explore North Holland from Amsterdam or from a host of smaller cities or villages in the province using either a car or a train. The possibilities are many. Generally speaking, comparable hotel accommodations cost less and are easier to find outside Amsterdam. Ask a VVV for advice. Since North Holland below the Noordzeekanaal (the canal that links Amsterdam with the North Sea) is for the most part firmly interwoven with that urban conglomeration called Rim City, you may prefer North Holland above the Noordzeekanaal where you'll find more open space.

Above the canal is a fine area to see the monuments of Holland's past: the windmills. From the 15th century on, windmills similar to the ones you'll see stood tall on the dikes. They helped create the polders you'll be looking at, by pumping lakes or marshes dry, and maintain the water level in the newly created polders by pumping excess water away. Other types of windmills were used to help saw wood, grind flour, or other

Many of Amsterdam's bridges, here at the junction of Leidschegracht and Herengracht, are illuminated all year. (Photo courtesy NBT)

tasks. If you look at almost any 17th-century landscape by one of Holland's "Golden Age" masters, you'll probably see at least one windmill in the painting.

With the arrival of steam- and electricity-powered machines, the wind-powered mills rapidly disappeared. Now, of a former total of 6,000 in the entire country, barely 1,000 remain. These windmills, which are registered as national

Amsterdam's Zuidertoren (South Tower), finished in 1614, is one of several in town with a carillon that is played regularly. (Photo courtesy NBT)

monuments, are owned and cared for by organizations like the Dutch Windmill Association, by a town or a village, and in rare instances by an individual. The mills' upkeep is subsidized by the national government. The mills are operated, most of the time, by members of the Guild of Volunteer Millers who passed a miller's exam. It's essential that windmills work regularly or they'll deteriorate; without the 700 licensed volunteer millers, the nation's precious windmill inventory would quickly disappear.

The ANWB has marked all the windmill monuments on its tourist maps with a windmill symbol. To see where the North Holland windmills "above the canal" are, look at ANWB tourist maps no. 1 (area north of Alkmaar) and no. 5 (area south of Alkmaar).

Choose a good windmill day (enough wind, but not too much) to visit windmill "De Kat." You can take the train from Amsterdam northwest to Uitgeest, where it's a 15-minute walk to the mill on the Geesterweg. The windmill pumps excess water out of the polder "De Zien" from the same spot where windmills have stood for 4 centuries.

Not all of the windmills you'll see in North Holland or elsewhere in The Netherlands function full-time or even part-time. Sometimes they turn just for Dutch schoolchildren or for tourists. One such windmill is the Museum Molen in Schermerhorn (the RH windmill on the cover of this book). In summer it works daily, wind permitting (except Mondays), pumping up and discarding the same recycled water for demonstration purposes. An English-speaking guide or a slide presentation in English can tell you about the history of the Dutch windmill and you may climb steep ladders to the top floor to see how the mill mechanism works from top to bottom. Drive to the mill, take a train to Alkmaar and rent a bicycle at the NS station, or take the regional bus 126 or 127 for Purmerend and get off at Noordervaart/Molendijk stop near Schermerhorn.

About 3 kilometers from the Museum Mill is Nic Jonk's sculpture garden. A collection of voluptuous bronze, mostly human figures is exhibited year-round in a very Dutch landscape of grass, reed-lined water, and faraway windmill silhouettes.

The North Sea coast dunes, part of which lie in the province of North Holland, are another kind of very Dutch landscape. You'll see the yellow strip mixed with green (for woods) on

Windmill De Kat, in Uitgeest, with sails stretched on its wings, is ready to work. Later, a volunteer miller rolls up a sail and swings it over for storage.

129

ANWB's tourist maps no. 1 and 5. The coastal dunes are vital to Holland's safety in protecting low-lying lands from assaults of the North Sea. The dunes also store drinking water for millions of Dutch. The water collects there after rain or snow or is pumped in from the Rhine or IJsselmeer, after being cleansed, of course. The dunes are mostly out of bounds to automobiles, but the map shows where you can drive to the inland edge of the dunes or through the dunes to the sea. To enjoy the dunes beyond a parking lot you can cycle along bicycle paths or walk on marked footpaths.

The Noordhollands Duinreservaat is easy to reach from the train station in Castricum and I have never known it to be crowded. Nature in this dune area is intimate and low-key. Wildflowers bloom along the paths and on the *speelweiden*, play areas, so marked. Rabbits race away among the low vegetation. They keep the sand dunes in top condition by nibbling away at grasses, just as the sheep in Drenthe eat the undesirable growth on the heather-covered heaths. A coot glides over a pond, watched by a blue crane standing regally on the shore. In a stand of conifers a cuckoo repeats its two-syllable call. Don't look south, or you may see beyond the idyllic setting of undulating dunes, of ponds and marshes, and spot the smoke-belching towers of the Hoogovens steel plant at the beginning of the Noordzeekanaal.

If architecture interests you, go back to the polderland and look at farms built in typical North Holland *stolpboerderij* style; sometimes people and cattle live together under one pyramid-shaped roof. Then there are the former Zuiderzee fishing villages of Marken and Volendam on the eastern coast. The villages are filled with tiny green-painted wooden houses with white trim; few residents still wear the traditional dress. The villages are nonetheless popular destinations on half-day bus tours from Amsterdam.

Two former Zuiderzee towns that once enjoyed a thriving international trade are Hoorn and Enkhuizen, which have preserved their handsome historic buildings. The open-air Zuiderzeemuseum in Enkhuizen is a village of traditional houses (including those in the style of Marken and Volendam) and mannequins wearing various types of traditional dress. At one house children may try on some of the clothes. In an indoor museum nearby, open all year, you can see fishing craft of the past. These towns are also on popular bus tours from Amsterdam.

Try to visit the town of Alkmaar on Fridays when an old market custom is called back to life. Pairs of men wearing white trousers and shirts and wide-brimmed straw hats like Venetian gondoliers carry piles of cheeses on stretchers between them to an ornately decorated 17th-century weighing house. Close by, the small Hans Brinker Museum is of interest if you've read Mary Mapes Dodge's tale of *Hans Brinker and the Silver Skates*. The museum curator can tell you what's true in the story and what isn't.

Spaarnedam is a village in a little rural pocket near Haarlem, and is below the Noordzeekanaal. You can drive there, or take a bus from Haarlem train station. The village is a *lintdorp* (ribbon village), meaning that the houses are strung along next to each other on both sides of a dike. You can buy smoked eel and a roll in an eel shop and sit down on the Spaarnedam dike.

A must in spring are the Keukenhof gardens near Haarlem. Nowhere else in the world will you be able to see such splendor of flowering tulips, daffodils, and hyacinths—with double

In Spaarnedam is this statue of the legendary boy who saved the country by sticking his finger in the dike. It is meant to "symbolize the perpetual struggle of Holland against the water."

This couple found a quiet spot to sun near a monument on the IJsselmeer dike south of Hoorn.

blooms, fringed petals, new colors, and variegated hues, all artfully planted under lovely old trees. A map of the 15-kilometer (10-mile) network of paths is for sale for 25 Dutch cents at the entrance. On fields outside Haarlem the bulbs also bloom, but there they are bunched together by color and kind in large rectangular patches and topped very quickly so the bulbs can retain their strength. The Keukenhof tour buses pass by the colored fields, and traffic may move slowly. I've enjoyed looking at the bulb fields from a train window or in combination with a trip above the Noordzeekanaal. You'll find bulb fields where you see little red tulips on your ANWB map no. 1.

If you want to study beach life in Holland, take the train on a warm holiday to Zandvoort on the west coast. The sandy beach will be jammed with sun worshippers and children playing in the sand or frolicking in the North Sea. Many women go topless; completely nude beaches also exist (look for the word *naaktstrand* on the map). The Zandvoort train will be crowded both ways, but driving is worse: on peak beach days the motor traffic may be stop-and-go all the way between Zandvoort and the German border.

Coastal Dunes Route from Castricum (about 26 km)

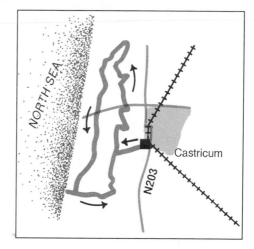

Additional route information: ANWB map no. 5 or map mentioned below.

Bicycle rental and starting point: NS station Castricum.

Route notes: Castricum is a 22-minute Intercity train ride from Amsterdam. Except for a short approach route from the station, the entire bicycle route is in the 5,000-hectare (12,500-acre) mostly car-free Noordhollands Duinreservaat. Stop at the VVV next to the Castricum station to buy an entrance ticket to the reserve and a *wandel- en fietskaart*, walking and cycling map, of the area if you don't have an ANWB map.

At the Johanna's Hof you can have a cup of coffee or a complete cooked meal. Don't take your rental bicycle on the beach (several of the beach accesses are paths of loose sand). Leave your bicycle in a nearby bicycle rack in the dunes, but don't forget to lock it.

Windmill Route from Alkmaar (about 30 km)

Additional route information: ANWB route map no. 1.

Bicycle rental and starting point: Alkmaar NS station.

Route notes: Alkmaar is a 30-minute Intercity train ride from Amsterdam. Pick up a local map at VVV

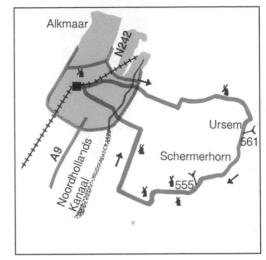

next to Alkmaar station to help you get out of the town. The bicycle route is entirely through flat polderland and likely to be windier than the previous ride. The Museum Mill is the middle of 3 in a row and well advertised with flags and signs and maybe tour buses. If possible, avoid Friday afternoons when tour buses stop at the mill after the Friday cheese market in Alkmaar. At the intersection Noordervaart/Molendijk, at ANWB signpost 555, turn right in the direction of Groot-Schermer for the Nic Jonk sculpture garden. It's on your left at signpost 561. On this route you'll pass close by at least 10 windmills with more mills at a distance, all pinpointed for you on ANWB map no. 1.

The ANWB *Fietsgids Noord-Holland/Noord* describes 2 Dijk-en-Duin (dike-and-dune) routes. You could ride no. 3, the 54-kilometer northern one from Den Helder (rent bicycle at NS station), or the 59-kilometer southern one, no. 5 out of Schagen, also on a train line from Amsterdam. (Three-speeds may not be available in Schagen.) Both routes are signed.

CHAPTER 11

Overijssel: Water, Woods, and Hanseatic Towns

Overijssel, as the name indicates, lies on the far side of the river IJssel when viewed from the west. The province can be divided into 3 main areas of interest: a waterlogged area that includes an outstanding wetlands reserve; two slightly hilly and occasionally wooded regions; and the IJssel towns.

For the waterlogged area in the far north of Overijssel you'll need ANWB tourist map no. 4 for Drenthe, or map no. 2 for Friesland. The wetlands reserve, Weerribben National Park, is former peat country. The subject of peat appears time and again in this book: the exploitation of peat affected the appearance of large portions of The Netherlands. For example, all those straight light blue lines in the Weerribben on the map were ditches left after peat was dug up. "The ditches filled up with water," explains a park docent, "and then plants started to grow, the beginning of a new habitat: reed beds. These are cut for commercial reasons (reed is used for the thatched roofs of Dutch farms and houses), but also for nature conservation. The ditches attract rare birds like bitterns, reed warblers, and purple herons."

You cannot drive through the park. At the north entrance in Ossenzijl is a visitors' center where you can obtain printed information in English, look at peat digging tools and photos of peat diggers, or watch a video, to date not with English commentary. A short walk along the Kalenbergsegracht, Kalenberg canal, brings you to a long row of year-round or second homes built along the canal. Several have thatched roofs, almost all are surrounded by lush-looking lawns and colorful flower beds. At the sides, the properties are separated from each other by narrow canals which are spanned by little humped bridges. You'll bounce over them like a yo-yo on a string on the Weerribben cycling route described below.

South of the Weerribben is De Wieden, a nature reserve that is also quite waterlogged and is more penetrable by car. Walk through the little town of Blokzijl (with probably the smallest locks you'll see in Holland) or Vollenhove (several historic buildings including a town hall now partially occupied by a restaurant).

Northeast and east of the Wieden are 2 popular tourist destinations, Giethoorn and Staphorst. They appear only on map no. 4. Giethoorn is called The Venice of Holland because the residents live on canals and transport themselves, their children, their groceries, and even their cows on shallow boats moved forward by pushing a long pole against the bottom of the canal. You can rent a punt and a pole and try this mode of locomotion or what's locally called a *fluisterboot* (a whisper boat, that is a row boat with an electric motor rather than a noisy and air-polluting gasoline one) to glide under Giethoorn's many bridges.

Staphorst is one of the few places left in The Netherlands where residents still wear traditional dress to please themselves, not to sell souvenirs or salted herring to tourists. The Staphorsters don't have much use for visitors, at least not when they take photos of them. If you want to see the Staphorster dress close up, go to the Museumboerderij, one of the farm museums.

For the rest of Overijssel you'll need ANWB tourist map no. 8, entitled Salland and Twente. These are the historic names of the 2 slightly hilly areas mentioned above. I have not been in Salland but can report on Twente, an area without marked boundaries that's shown in capital letters on the map south of Almelo. The Romans called it Tubantia, still the name of a Twente newspaper.

In Twente, as in Gelderland's Achterhoek, you see *houtwallen*, walls of wood, that separate the cultivated fields or the meadows from each other. In their purest form, the *houtwallen* are made of birches and oaks, their low branches braided together. Every 10 years a *houtwal* is cut down to allow young shoots to branch out. *Houtwallen* are now mainly preserved as natural historical monuments.

The designer of the ***Hotel De Lutt (in De Lutte near Oldenzaal) borrowed architectural designs from the so-called Saxon farmhouses typical of Twente. The lower parts of the outside walls of this small country hotel are brick, the upper parts vertical unpainted oak slabs that have taken on a rich weathered look. The deep roof is red-tiled and topped by a slender wooden gable sign, at least 1 meter high, made of oak and showing from the bottom up: 2 half moons, a symbol of the sun, an ear of wheat, and a cross. Traditionally such a gable sign is meant to drive evil spirits away.

One of Twente's attractions close to De Lutte is an arboretum established in 1910 by one of the leaders of Twente's former textile industry: 900 trees, shrubs, and bushes, all properly identified, are now fully grown and look particularly splendid in spring or fall.

This car ferry goes back and forth across Zwarte Water near Zwartesluis.

Attendant in the Museumboerderij "Oud Staphorst" shows off the pleating of a woolen skirt worn by Staphorst women.

The textile barons built handsome mansions, several of which you will pass in your Twente travels. The mansion in Denekamp is near a famous waterwheel mill that daily saws wood for show and is a popular tour bus destination. In the town of Ootmarsum the VVV offers a folder in English describing a walk past restored old houses and a church with remarkable treasures. A slide show tells you about old Twente customs observed at times of year you are not likely to be there (December: blowing a big horn over a well to celebrate the birth of Christ; Easter: bonfires to celebrate His resurrection).

In summer the temperatures in Overijssel's Twente and Salland, as in Gelderland's Achterhoek, are likely to be a few degrees higher and the wind is likely to blow less than, for example, in the maritime provinces along the North Sea. But with the fickle Dutch weather there are no guarantees. I've had good weather in May and September; I found Twente an area of soothing calm.

The IJssel towns of Overijssel are Kampen, Zwolle, and Deventer. These are historic towns with walls, monumental gates, and impressive town halls. The 3 towns were all members of the Hansa, the medieval league of principally German towns that promoted and protected trading privileges.

Kampen stretches out along the IJssel where sailing ships once moored. Some of the streets in Kampen haven't changed since the town's heyday: short narrow streets lead at right angles to the once all-important river quays. The people of Kampen sailed along rivers to towns in the west and in the German Rhineland. They also made dangerous sea voyages around Denmark through the Sont channel to reach German towns on the Baltic Sea. For 2 centuries Kampen had trade relations all over Europe, which sometimes resulted in exotic gifts, such as the 2 live lions Lisbon sent to Kampen in 1477. Kampen's trade declined when the Danes started levying ever higher tolls for the privilege of sailing through the Sont. Other foreign markets opened up, but by then upstart Amsterdam had cornered them.

Zwolle, situated on a short side arm of the IJssel, also thrived on trade, but its hinterland didn't go much farther than Twente, Salland, and western Germany. Danish oxen were traded in Zwolle after having been walked for several hundred kilometers from Denmark through Northern Germany and what are now the provinces of Groningen and Drenthe. En

The Singraven mansion in Denekamp is open to the public.

Main canal in Weerribben national park draws cyclists and an angler prepared for rain.

route the emaciated animals were fattened up at rest meadows. It is said that 20,000 oxen were marched to Zwolle and eventually to other West European markets in one year, around 1500. Reminders of Zwolle's days of prosperity include the Gothic St. Michael's church with an organ that has 4,000 pipes and is considered one of the most beautiful in Holland. It was designed by Arp Schnitger and completed by his sons Frans-Caspar and Jurien in 1721.

The merchants of Deventer, instead of sending their own ships to faraway places to fetch the goods, let others do this and traded the wares brought in at international markets held 5 times a year. In the 14th and 15th centuries these were among the most important markets in Europe. On waterways and overland came iron and copper, nitric acid to make explosives, rye, bacon, cloth, herrings, cheese and butter, furs, and wine. During 3 months recorded in 1466–1467, more than half the ships that passed Cologne on the Rhine towards the Low Countries carried barrels of wine. Some barrels were also

Cycling Holland's backroads may include waterway crossings on a ferry so small that the ferryman transports bike and cyclist separately. This one is in the Wieden area of Overijssel.

floated downstream on rafts that were sold along with the wine at the end of the trip. Timber was an important commodity—to build houses, ships, and those edifices of prestige, churches.

Some of the Deventer churches remain. The Lebüinus church was started as a Romanesque church in 1040 and was completed with a Gothic addition in the mid-17th century. In the tower hang 47 bells of the oldest carillon made by the Hemony brothers. The medieval street pattern of Deventer remains virtually unchanged, and houses in the 13th-century quarter have been restored.

Weerribben Route from Steenwijk (about 40 km)

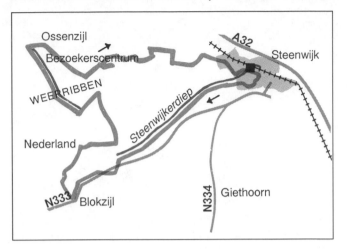

Additional route information: ANWB tourist maps no. 2 or 4. Route overlaps the ANWB Weeribben route, no. 19 described in ANWB *Fietsgids Friesland*, so you'll see red-on-white hexagonal ANWB shields marked Weerribben most of the way.

Bicycle rental and starting point: NS station Steenwijk.

Hotel: ***De Gouden Engel, a short cycle ride from the station.

Route notes: In mid-April a friend and I left the station in flurries of wet snow, were pelted by hail in the Weerribben National Park, but also had some sunshine. There were no other recreational cyclists.

After Molenhoek (ANWB map shows a *klokkestoel* symbol) the ANWB route dips down to the Steenwijkerdiep, and then up to Steenwijk, but we made a more direct line for Steenwijk. This is one of my favorite rides. The path along the Kalenberger canal with the many humped bridges, the colorful gardens, and the houses with thatched roofs, you'll see nowhere else.

Gildehaus-Dinkel Route from De Lutte (about 30 km)

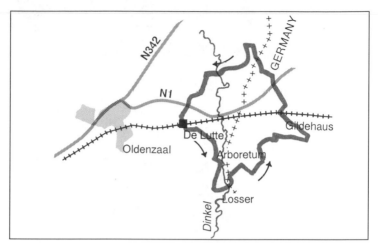

This route crosses the Dutch-German border to go to Gildehaus in Germany. The winding Dinkel is a river described in tourist literature as "the most idyllic little river" in The Netherlands.

Additional route information: ANWB tourist map no. 8. A similar route is included in the *Fietsgids Twente/Salland*, no. 19. The ANWB route is signed.

Starting point and hotel: ***Hotel De Lutt. Take the train to Oldenzaal and a taxi to the hotel, or make arrangements with the hotel to be picked up.

Bicycles: Available at hotel.

Route notes: This route has 2 "green" border crossings (crossings without customs people to ask for your passport, but carry yours anyway). On the way out you know you are in Germany because the name of a riding school and a restaurant you pass are in German. On the way back a tiny sign tells you that you are entering Nederland. Part of this route goes over a bikeway in the Bentheimer woods, erstwhile domain of the counts of Bentheim. In Germany you cycle up the Mühlenberg (*Mühle*, windmill, is on top) and you can sit on a bench and overlook Holland's neighbor. Return is via Lutterzand, where the Dinkel has hollowed out its shores so much that roots of trees dangle in space above the water.

The Natura Docet (nature teaches) museum in Denekamp is just one of hundreds of small museums in The Netherlands.

Hotel De Lutt has other suggestions for local cycling, in English.

Of the 20 routes in the ANWB *Fietsids Twente/Salland*, 16 are signed. A few of these can also be reached from De Lutte, such as the Springendal route, no. 17, that includes Ootmarsum and Denekamp.

CHAPTER 12

South Holland: Green Oases amid Urban Growth

"Zuid-Holland is groot in groen," South Holland is great in green, is the title of a recent publication of the provincial information bureau. The brochure is meant to remind the Dutch that besides the well-known big cities and much-visited museums, the province has "little-known green areas and footpaths and bikeways away from motorized traffic."

This sculpture of a Scheveningen fisherwoman commemorates lives of fishermen lost at sea.

In this green heart of the province, set aside by law to ensure breathing space for the ever-growing South Holland population, you can see the same polder landscape as in North Holland. You could drive, for example, to the area around the Nieuwkoopse Plassen east of Alphen a/d Rijn (a/d stands for "on the," and the Rhine here is called Oude Rijn, Old Rhine). You'll need ANWB tourist map no. 6 to chart your route. Be sure to include roads traced with green on the ANWB map

since green means "scenic." But when the weather is nice and it's a weekend or holiday, these rural roads may be crowded with Dutch out for a drive.

If historic towns are on your agenda, try Oudewater (pop. 10,000), which actually lies just east of South Holland in Utrecht province, or Gouda (pop. 63,000). In Oudewater you can go to the 16th-century *Waag*, weighing house, on the Havenstraat and see a copy of scales used to weigh those accused of being witches or sorcerers. If their weight was "in accordance with the natural proportions of the body" they were obviously too heavy to fly on a broomstick and thus saved from death at the stake. Next to the weighing house you can visit the step-gabled house of Arminius (1560-1609). This Dutch theologian did not concur with the Calvinist leaders of his day and endured years of mutual discord and hatred. His beliefs later formed the base of doctrines embraced by the Methodist church.

Pedestrian ferry crossing the IJssel between Zwolle and Hattem.

Gouda has one of the most photogenic Gothic town halls in The Netherlands. You'll find the small hall on the market square (market day is Friday). On the left of the building, when you face the entrance, is a tiny automatic carillon that plays a melody every half hour as little porcelain figures become visible and depict Floris V, count of Holland, bestowing town privileges on Gouda in 1272. St. John is an enormous church with famous stained-glass windows. Inquire ahead when the church is open to visitors. You can reach Gouda by train and Oudewater by train and bus.

With a car you can also go to the Krimpenerwaard or the Alblasserwaard regions. *Waard* means land enclosed by rivers, in this case the Hollandsche IJssel (not the same IJssel as in Overijssel), the Lek (a new name for the Rhine as it courses towards the North Sea), and the Waal (a branch of the Rhine). Here you'll find yet more thoroughly Dutch polder landscapes

The pedestrian ferry Vice Versa plies the river Lek between Krimpen a/d Lek and the windmills of Kinderdijk. (Photos courtesy Vrienden van de

and some delightful roads that skirt a canal or a river. Some of these roads are marked with green on the ANWB tourist map.

At Kinderdijk, in the west of the Alblasserwaard, is one of Holland's most popular tourist sights, 19 windmills in a cozy little group together, once used to pump up water and now maintained as national monuments. The mills operate Saturday afternoons in the summer. On other days one windmill is usually in operation and open to the public.

To reach Kinderdijk from the north, take the car ferry across the Lek in Krimpen a/d Lek. You can also park your car there

Poplars mirrored in Aarkanaal north of Alphen a/d Rijn. (Photo Frits Weideman)

and take the *voetveer* (pedestrian ferry) for pedestrians and cyclists which goes to Kinderdijk with a stop at Slikkerveer. You'll have to walk approximately 10 minutes from the ferry landing at Kinderdijk to the windmills. On your ANWB map, car ferries are marked with a double thin black line and pedestrian ferries with a single line.

A Dutch pedestrian ferry is either a rowboat rowed by a ferryman, a raft pulled by him along a rope, a motorized raft, or a motorboat. Most of the 60 *voetveren* still extant in The Netherlands are now motorized. Some pedestrian ferries keep regular schedules, others are on call. If you want to cross, wave to someone at the other side or ring a bell. About a third of all Dutch pedestrian ferries are in the province of South Holland.

For more touring in the countryside, go to South Holland's dunes. You can reach them via roads that go through the dunes all the way to the sea boulevard in Noordwijk, Katwijk, Wassenaar, Scheveningen, and Kijkduin. Take a walk in the dunes or walk along the sandy beach and soak up the salty North Sea air. On a warm day the beach will be covered with sunbathers, but the density tends to decrease rapidly farther away from the parking lot.

If you want a change from polders and dunes, there are South Holland's cities. The 2 largest are The Hague, with museums and stately historic buildings, and Rotterdam, with its enormous port. You can take a boat trip through the port, passing kilometers-long container quays and freighters flying flags from many countries. To see some of the action in a different way, you can drive to a restaurant that overlooks the Nieuwe Waterweg, over which huge cargo ships and an occasional cruise ship reach the North Sea. Try the ****Delta Hotel in Vlaardingen

For a similar experience elsewhere, try De Kop van de Haven in IJmuiden, North Holland. From a window here you can almost touch the giant vessels squeezing through the Noordzeekanaal in or out of the IJmuiden locks. From the restaurant of ****Hotel Britannia or other boulevard restaurants in Vlissingen (see the Zeeland chapter) you may see giant ships entering or leaving the Western Scheldt. The ****Rijn Hotel in Arnhem (see the Gelderland chapter) also offers good

*Venerable town halls come in many sizes. This petite one is in Naaldwijk,
South Holland. (Photo courtesy NBT)*

river views. However, river traffic is rarely as impressive as
those castles of container ships that ply the oceans of the world.

Here follows a suggestion for seeing Holland's "green heart"
on a bicycle. As in North Holland, you can easily reach the
beginning of a bicycle route by car, train, or bus from almost
anywhere in the province and have time to return to your base
at night.

Meije Route from Alphen a/d Rijn (about 55 km)

Bicycle rental and starting point: NS station Alphen a/d Rijn.

Route notes: The highlight of this route is the bikeway across the Zuideinderplas where you cycle on a narrow strip of land with water and boats on both sides. On the road to Nieuwkoop turn right at ANWB signpost 4190 (do not go

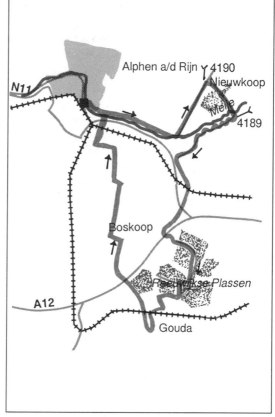

into Nieuwkoop, the road is narrow with many parked and moving vehicles), cycle as far as the water tower at signpost 4189 in Meije village, and turn right. This path once was a *kerkepad* for churchgoers, also called the *Oortjespad*: Catholics going to church in Nieuwkoop could use the path gratis, non-Catholics had to pay an *oortje* (1¼ cents). Do not take the scenic narrow winding road along the Meije (water on both sides) at a time of day when motor traffic will be heavy.

This *Oortjespad* is also part of the 44-kilometer Nieuwkoopse Plassen route, no. 5 in the ANWB *Fietsgids Zuid-Holland/Noord*. The route, which is unsigned, includes Aarlanderveen windmills and leaves from Alphen a/d Rijn.

Two signed ANWB routes described in the *Fietsgids Zuid-Holland/Zuid* , also in the green heart, are 46-kilometer Zuiderplaspolder route, no. 5, and Krimpenerwaard route, no. 6, both out of Gouda with NS station bicycle rental (only standard bicycles). If you need a town map to reach your route or other information, the Gouda VVV is a short walk from the station on the market square with the photogenic town hall. Route no. 6 passes the new ****Hotel de Aarendshoeve in Bergambacht, right in the polder next to windmill De Aarend (on the map). You can stop here for refreshments or stay overnight (bus from Gouda) and start cycling from the hotel. The hotel loans bicycles to guests and offers several bicycle route suggestions in English. Farther on the route you pass Krimpen a/d Lek, where you can take the foot ferry to the Kinderdijk windmills. As your ANWB map will show, there are plenty of other windmills around as well.

CHAPTER 13

Utrecht:
Palaces and Mansions

Just as there are 2 Groningens in The Netherlands, a city and a province, so there are 2 Utrechts. The appropriate ANWB tourist map for both is no. 6; you'll also need no. 7 for the far eastern section of the province and no. 5 for a tiny northwestern section.

The city of Utrecht is one of Holland's major cities (pop. 231,000), with Hoog Catharijne, the largest shopping complex in the country, housed in an annex to the largest railway station in the country, and a wealth of museums and old churches. The province of Utrecht, on the other hand, is the smallest of the 12 provinces. Its small size encompasses every type of landscape in The Netherlands except coastal dunes. If you are short on time, you could drive or cycle a backroad loop around the city of Utrecht and see these landscapes in a day or two.

You should know, however, that all of the province of Utrecht is either part of or adjacent to Rim City. Between natural areas set aside as preserves and rural areas designated to remain rural, a lot of construction is going on. A lovely pastoral view in the flatland or a view from Utrecht's Heuvelrug, Ridge of Hills, may be marred by a freeway in the making, by a new factory, or by an office highrise.

Following are some places you might want to include in a clockwise loop around the city of Utrecht. Amersfoort (pop. 100,000) is another of Holland's historic towns with a double moat, stone walls and gates, and a well-preserved or restored center. The town, northeast of Utrecht, is home to the Bei-aardschool, Carillon School. On Thursday evenings and Friday mornings you can hear student recitals on the 47-bell 17th-century Hemony carillon in the freestanding Onze Lieve Vrouwe Toren, Tower of our Lady (the church accidentally blew up a few centuries ago). Students also practice or play on the modern carillon of the Belgian Monument, a Belgian gift of thanks for Dutch help during the First World War, and a 15-minute bus or bicycle ride from downtown. The school itself is not open to the public except in July and August on VVV-organized Historic Amersfoort walks.

Den Treek-Henschoten, a green area on the map south of Amersfoort, is a public park. You'll see many beautiful beeches on the grounds of this former private estate. The owner's country home has become **Huize "Den Treek," where you can have a cup of tea on the spacious lawn near a pond, enjoy a meal in the Specialties Restaurant, or spend the night in one of the hotel rooms, not all of which have private amenities.

Outside the town of Maarsbergen is the Kaas en Museum Boerderij (Cheese and Museum Farm), known as "De Wei-staar." Order a sandwich with the farm's *boerenkaas*, farmer's cheese, or buy a porcelain milk jug in the shape of a cow (the blue designs look like real Delft, but are not).

In Doorn is the palace where, after the First World War, the German Emperor Wilhelm II lived in exile from 1920 until his death in 1941. You can see art treasures from German imperial palaces including a collection of snuff boxes and watches from Frederick the Great, King of Prussia (1712–1786).

South of Doorn you are in polderland and, as indicated by the symbols on the ANWB map, in a land of castles and mansions. Few of them, however, are open to the public. A good castle route is the road along the Langbroeker Wetering, then south to the river Lek, which is the name the (Neder) Rijn takes on at Wijk-bij-Duurstede.

Wijk-bij-Duurstede (pop. 15,500) is another small Dutch town with a history of ups and downs: first a Roman defense post, then a center of river trade, it was later devastated by the Vikings and inundated by floods. After Wijk received town rights, it flourished again as a trade center and as the residence of a Utrecht bishop who brought in artists and scientists. In the 20th century new people came for the quiet of Wijk and its historic atmosphere. Newcomers include Kees and Willie van de Dood, a husband and wife team who restore pianos, particularly German ones made between 1900 and 1940, and polish them, using a 500-year-old process. After the wood has been sanded smooth as a miror, all its pores closed, Kees or Willie apply several layers of a shellac/alcohol mixture with a wad of wool wrapped in linen or cotton. You are welcome to watch this process in their workshop at Wilhelminastraat 2, but call ahead.

Near Wijk's windmill, which occasionally grinds wheat into flour, is the restaurant 't Schippershuys (the Skipper's House) at Dijkstraat 5. The restaurant often serves meals across the street on a terrace on the dike; I had a large platter of smoked salmon here and a very thin French pancake for dessert. Near the terrace is an old *waterpoort*, water gate, in the dike. When the river water started to rise, men used to hoist

Poffertjes, tiny pancakes, prepared at one of the many summer fairs held in Utrecht and elsewhere.

beams horizontally into slots at the sides of the *poort*, one on top of the other, and then lean sandbags against the beams. Later, steel doors were closed hydraulically. The Dutch have since rearranged the waterways and now there's a meadow behind the dike. A short walk will bring you to the Amsterdam-Rijn Kanaal, one of the busiest waterways in western Europe.

After Wijk-bij-Duurstede, travel west through Nieuwegein, earmarked for building growth, to the Lopikerwaard. Here you can drive the Lek dike road, marked in green on the ANWB map for scenic. When you plan to drive or cycle along a dike be aware that the road may not run on top of the dike, offering a view on either side, but at the bottom and inside of the dike so you can only see the polder. For a look at the river, canal, or lake, you may have to climb stairs to the top of the dike. ANWB may have marked viewpoints for you on the map with the international view sign, a half circle of red rays.

If you drive or cycle to the very west of the Lopikerwaard you reach the province of South Holland, and, heading north, one of Holland's most renowned scenic roads along the river Vlist. The map marks this route with scenic green on both sides; the eastern side is usually less crowded. From the Vlist you can go to Haastrecht (a small historic town with a handsome town hall), then east to Oudewater, already mentioned in the South Holland chapter, and Woerden, a large cheese center. Return to the province of Utrecht at Harmelen.

From Harmelen you can go north to Breukelen via either Haarzuilens or Kamerik. Castle de Haar in Haarzuilens has all the elements of a medieval castle, including a moat and turrets, but was built at the end of the 19th century. Some Dutch irreverently call the present castle, which was built on the ruins of an earlier castle, a *nepkasteel*, a fake castle, others use the word neo-castle.

The road through Kamerik runs with the Kamerikse Wetering at your left and at your right a *sloot* (small drainage canal) with little bridges over it to the homes at the other side. This is a very Dutch scene, and you'll probably love it. You may not be so enamored of the road: It's narrow, at several places too narrow for cars to pass each other, so when you meet another car you may be the one who has to back up into a passing zone or edge over to the shoulder to make room. As a driver or cyclist totally unfamiliar with the road and the firmness of the shoulder, and certainly not used to sharing a narrow road with water on both sides with motorists zipping along, you may wish to avoid this route. You might settle for the N212, located just a bit to the east. This is a proper 2-lane highway, and has a roadside bicycle path. Then again, the Kamerikse Wetering

Utrecht city's dom, cathedral, towers over trees and a statue honoring victims of World War II.

road is more of a challenge and gives a better close-up view of Holland; try it in the early morning, perhaps, when the traffic is lighter.

After Breukelen you travel a road north along the Vecht, marked again by ANWB with scenic green. On the shores of the river are villas and mansions, some with *theekoepels*, tea domes with walls, where ladies entertained guests for tea. Turn right at the Bloklaan and you will enter a different type of landscape, the Loosdrechtse Plassen, Loosdrecht Lakes. These are peat lakes, formed after peat was dug up, but not later drained as other peat lakes were. The lakes attract water-sports fans and, as you cross the causeway, you see the white and colored sails of boats and windsurf boards. To avoid Hilversum (pop. 85,000) on your way back to Amersfoort you can return to the Loosdrechtse Plassen and encircle the Breu-keleveense Plas and go east again via Tienhoven, Westbroek, and Maartensdijk, then north into a green area called De Vuursche.

The woods in De Vuursche are the most-visited in the country. The National Forest Service has stimulated recreation with good access roads, large parking lots, picnic areas, and a miniature golf course near Lage Vuursche village, and cut down on amenities elsewhere, for example in the nature pre-serve De Stulp. This keeps most people away and provides more quiet for plants and animals. De Stulp is not named on the ANWB tourist map, but lies east of Lage Vuursche, colored in pink and green.

Return to Amersfoort via Soestdijk for a look at the white palace where Princess (formerly Queen) Juliana lives with her husband Prince Bernard, parents of the present Queen Beatrix. This entire itinerary covers under 200 kilometers (120 miles).

I cycled this loop in 4 days in May 1990, starting in Amersfoort where I rented a bicycle at the NS station. The 3 hotels where I had made reservations and which I enjoyed were:

Wijk-bij-Duurstede: ***Hotel-Restaurant De Oude Lantaarn is an old inn off the cobbled market square. In 1990 this was the only hotel in town.

Harmelen: ***Het Wapen van Harmelen is a solidly Dutch country hotel. Rooms in the rear overlook meadows and the Old Rhine, already shriveled up to the size of a *sloot*. Front rooms overlook a church flanked by an enormous chestnut tree which in May gloriously bloomed, and a main thorough-fare which may be noisy early in the morning as trucks pass by with flowers for the auction in Aalsmeer.

Lage Vuursche: ***Restaurant-Hotel De Kastanjehof, an *à la carte* restaurant with hotel accommodations, is surrounded by woods. It is the cuisine that really matters to the management; the rooms are mainly there for those who don't want to drive after a copious dinner with wines. My room was tastefully done and looked out over a garden with flowering chestnut trees.

You can add a loop from Amersfoort to Spakenburg and back, another 30 or so kilometers, that passes through the Eempolder (Eemland on map). This area is slated for a very Dutch kind of overhaul called *ruilverkaveling*, land reappor-tionment. Because farmers now live far from their land (by Dutch standards), new farms will be built for them along with new or widened roads, and small scattered pieces of a farmer's land will be exchanged for one large section so he can work his property with modern machines. In this small and crowded country there's nary a piece of nature, cultivated or wild, that has not been rearranged in an effort to increase the quality of life for the people.

Spakenburg used to be located on the Zuiderzee, and for centuries local fishermen sailed out to the Zuiderzee to catch saltwater fish. Now Spakenburg lies on the Eemmeer, Lake Eem, one of the border lakes of Flevoland, and fishermen sail out to Lake IJssel for freshwater fish, notably eel. On "Spaken-burg days," two Wednesdays in July and August, most wom-en wear their traditional dress. Ask their permission before you photograph them.

Valleikanaal Route from Amersfoort (about 32 km)

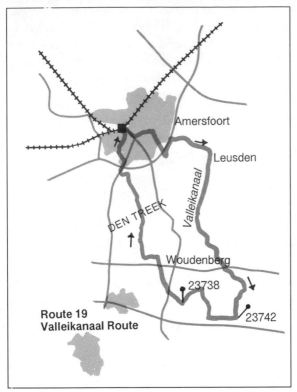

Additional route information: ANWB tourist maps nos. 6 and 7.

Bicycle rental and starting point: NS station Amersfoort.

Route notes: Ask the VVV Amersfoort, opposite NS station, how to reach the Valleikanaal. A bikeway away from cars parallels the canal for about 10 kilometers. At ANWB signpost 23742 turn right onto the road along the railroad line, make another right at signpost 23741, then turn left at Rottegatsteeg. The cheese farm is on your left (closed Sundays). In the Den Treek park you again cycle on a bikeway. This is an easy and well-protected route.

CHAPTER 14

Zeeland: Showcase of Water Control

Half a century ago the province of Zeeland consisted of islands that floated like pieces of a jigsaw puzzle in the arms of the North Sea. Linked to other Dutch provinces only by ferries and by one roundabout railroad line, the province was isolated from the rest of the nation. Then came the storm of 1953. The sea breached dikes and flooded parts of the islands of Zeeland and parts of South Holland to the north.

The Eastern Scheldt barrier, completed in 1986, links Zeeland with the rest of the country.

Over 1,800 people drowned, 200,000 horses, cows, pigs, sheep, and chickens perished, and 47,000 buildings were damaged or completely destroyed. Farmland was ruined for years to come by the salt of the sea.

To make sure that such a flood could never happen again, government engineers designed the Delta Plan. Delta refers here to the area enclosed by the rivers Rhine, Meuse, and Scheldt as they empty into the North Sea. Most of the sea arms in South Holland and Zeeland are now closed off with dams, and the extensive coastlines of the islands are no longer exposed to threats of the sea. Only the Nieuwe Waterweg, the "mouth of the Rhine," passing by the port of Rotterdam, and the Western Scheldt are left open for big ships to go in and out. The Western Scheldt provides North Sea access for Belgium's port of Antwerp.

Zeeland is isolated no more. Atop the Delta Plan dams are highways and bicycle paths over which you can travel directly and speedily to the (former) islands of Zeeland. Such a journey could well be a highlight of your trip to The Netherlands. The Dutch have been fighting the water of rivers and sea for 2,000 years, and it's in Zeeland that the Dutch can finally say that they have won their seemingly endless battle. To stand on a dam of the Delta Plan and to see one of the latest engineering works close up is, in a small way, to become part of this Dutch victory.

For a trip through Zeeland, you'd need ANWB tourist map no. 10. If you come from the north via the most western route, N57, you will first cross the 4.5-kilometer Haringvlietdam, which links the 2 South Holland islands of Voorne-Putten and Goeree-Overflakkee. Next you will travel over the 6-kilometer Brouwersdam, completed in 1972, linking Goeree-Overflak-kee with Schouwen-Duiveland in Zeeland. The third dam on this route is the 9-kilometer Oosterscheldekering, Eastern Scheldt barrier, completed in 1986. It connects Schouwen-Duiveland with Noord-Beveland and is sometimes called the "dam of reconciliation" because it came about after political and environmental debates that went on for 7 years.

To learn more about the sophisticated technology used by the engineers of Rijkswaterstaat, visit the Delta-Expo exhibit on Neeltje Jans, a work platform established when the Ooster-scheldekering was under construction. You can reach Neeltje Jans by car or by public transportation. Take the roundabout train, via North Brabant, to Middelburg on Walcheren (2½ hours from Amsterdam), then bus no. 104 from the train station to Neeltje Jans (25 minutes). Service is hourly. You can also join an organized bus tour from one of a number of places in The Netherlands. This will cost more than public transportation, but an English-speaking guide will take care of you for the day. I've described a bicycle tour at the end of this chapter.

Continuing south from Delta-Expo you'll cross one more Delta Plan dam, the 6-kilometer Veersegatdam, completed in 1961. It links Noord-Beveland with the former islands of Walcheren and Zuid-Beveland.

The southernmost part of Zeeland is called Zeeuwsch-Vlaanderen or Zeeland-Flanders (there's also a Belgian Flanders) and borders on Belgium. You'll now need ANWB tourist map no. 12. On it the historic spelling of Zeeuwsch-Vlaanderen

This monumental town gate once was part of Zierikzee's defense system.

with its silent *ch* has been modernized to Zeeuws-Vlaanderen. To reach Zeeuwsch-Vlaanderen take a car ferry from either Vlissingen (Flushing in English) or Kruiningen. The crossing takes 20 minutes.

Zeeland's capital Middelburg (pop. 40,000) is a good central point from which to explore Zeeland. The town itself is rich in monuments: 1,100 are on the national monument list, many restored after destruction in the beginning of the Second World War when the Germans bombed Middelburg. The 86-meter abbey tower, which the Middelburgers affectionately call Lange Jan, "Tall John," is such a monument. Climb it, and from the top see the star-shaped moat so typical of fortified towns in the Middle Ages. The tower's carillon of 49 bells plays every quarter hour, or catch a noon concert by the town's carillonneur, usually on Thursday. The 12th-century abbey complex has a cobbled square of great dignity and a surround of cloisters where you expect any time to see a medieval monk in homespun habit coming towards you reading his handwritten book.

Also of interest in Middelburg is the Roosevelt Study Center. The Roosevelt family came from Oud Vossemeer on Tholen. There's an exhibition on Theodore, Franklin D., and Eleanor, and 3,000 books and documents for anyone interested in 20th-century American history. The Franklin and Eleanor Roosevelt Institute here promotes the principles essential to democracy with the annual Franklin D. Roosevelt Four Freedoms Awards. In 1990 one of the recipients of the Four Freedoms Medal was Václav Havel, playwright and President of the Czech and Slovak Federal Republic.

Across from the Roosevelt Center is the Zeeland Museum, small if you compare it with the Rijksmuseum, the National Gallery, in Amsterdam, but the right size to see everything at your ease in one visit. Five enormous wall tapestries, woven in the early 17th century, show sea battles of the province of Zeeland (it was one of the 7 that formed the Dutch Republic) in the Eighty Years War against Spain, the Dutch war of independence, 1568–1648. A smaller tapestry depicts the coat of arms of Zeeland. In the center you see a shield with a swimming heraldic lion and underneath the words *Luctor et Emergo*, I struggle and emerge.

The museum has a remarkable collection of votive altars dating from the 3rd century A.D. and dedicated to a goddess called Nehalennia. These altars are decorative tablets or statues that were made to order for Roman traders who had asked for Nehalennia's protection on a business trip to Brittannia, vowing to pay her tribute with an altar if they safely returned. The altars are usually inscribed, in Latin, with the name of the goddess (who is assumed to have been a local one, since no mention of her is made elsewhere in the Roman Empire), and that of the donor or donors and sometimes their merchandise (salt, earthenware). These altars were uncovered after a storm on a sandy beach near Domburg on Walcheren in 1674 or are copies of some of the 140 other altars that were found later. The originals are displayed in the Rijksmuseum voor Oudheden, National Museum of Archeology, in Leiden.

This Roman limestone sculpture representing the goddess Nehalennia was fished up from the Eastern Scheldt in 1971. A copy is on display at Zeeland Museum.

165

There are other sights to visit outside Middelburg besides Delta-Expo. Six kilometers northeast of Middelburg is the little town of Veere (pop. 5,000) with an inn in the Campveerse Toren (tower). In 1575 William of Orange arranged for a wedding dinner at the inn after one of his marriages. Along the coast of Walcheren are dunes and North Sea beaches you can drive or cycle along. In the 19th century, Domburg was a posh resort and royalty of Europe came here to breathe the healthy sea air. The once chic Bad Hotel now stands empty waiting for money to restore it to its former opulence or to be demolished by a wrecker.

A trip south of Middelburg to Vlissingen and a ferry ride over the Western Scheldt brings you to Breskens in Zeeuwsch-Vlaanderen. Some Dutch say that the people here are more Belgian than Dutch and that they don't take life as seriously as their countrymen north of the Western Scheldt do. True or not, shops in Zeeuwsch-Vlaanderen are open on Sundays and so are cafés. Zeeuwsch-Vlaanderen is polder country, but dozens of *kreken*, creeks, left over from a sea arm or a river wind through the rectangular landscape and lend charm to it. Some of the *kreken* are part of nature preserves near Nieuwvliet and Oostburg.

On Schouwen-Duiveland, some 40 kilometers from Middelburg, after going north over the beautiful sweep of the 5-kilometer-long Zeelandbrug, is Zierikzee (pop. 10,000). This is a tourist mecca for its protected town views and historic facades, and perhaps for its very own delicacy, *palingbrood*, eel bread. To prepare this dish, raw eel is folded into the dough of an oblong roll and baked with the roll. When the roll comes out of the oven, crisp and golden brown, it's permeated by the fragrance of eel. Be careful: the bones are still in the eel and you should eat the roll sideways, as if you were playing a harmonica or mouth organ.

All over Zeeland you can eat Zeeland oysters. Their quality is rated by zero's; the *principalen* rate the highest with six 0's. Oysters are available fresh from September to March. Mussels, the "poor man's oysters," are available fresh from July to March, and frozen in other months. For a Zeeland sweet, try a freshly made *bolus*, a saucer-shaped sugarcoated pastry made from flour, milk, butter, egg, and yeast, available in many a Zeeland bakery, or *roomboterbabbelaars,* a hard candy made of sugar and butter. These are often packed in tins with a picture of a young girl in one of the now rarely seen regional dresses. This treat is also sold in some candy shops outside the province.

Some complain that now that Zeeland is connected with the rest of the Dutch nation all those cars bring fumes and noise and crowds. The crowds come to the new lakes, the Veersemeer and the Grevelingenmeer, to surf, sail, swim, scuba dive, and play, and to the sandy North Sea beaches of Schouwen-Duiveland, Walcheren, and Zeeuwsch-Vlaanderen. They stay in a campsite, a bungalow park, or a seaside hotel. But they usually do not move far from the parking lots of popular resorts and recreation areas, and they come mainly in summer and during long holiday weekends.

I was last in Zeeland in the middle of April. The Walcheren farmers had just plowed their fields and the earth lay bare, reddish brown, in pleasing patterns of straight lines and graceful curves, without a wrinkle or a bump. Poplars on the dikes were in their spring color of yellow. I found Zeeland's countryside appealing and I saw very few other tourists about.

The Latin motto on a windmill at Hulst, Zeeuwsch Vlaanderen, translates as "small things grow through harmony."

Tilting the ring is a favorite summer activity in some Zeeland villages. This event was photographed in Biggekerke on the island of Walcheren.

The 2 Zeeland hotels at which I stayed are in Middelburg: the new ****Arneville, on the outskirts of town, a short walk or taxi ride from the railroad station, and the older ***Hotel du Commerce. This hotel is opposite the railway station separated from it by a canal. On your way to or from the train you may find yourself standing in a throng of cyclists waiting patiently for the canal bridge to let a barge or yacht sail through.

Walcheren Route from Middelburg (about 35 km and 40 km optional extension)

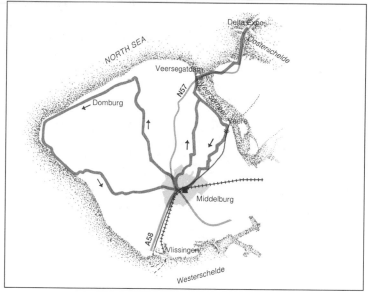

Additional route information: ANWB map no. 10.

Bicycle rental: NS station Middelburg.

Starting point: ****Hotel Arneville.

Parent with two children on one bike epitomizes the Dutch approach to cycling, here in the tranquillity of the coastal dunes.

Route notes: Part of this route follows the signed Manteling-en route, no. 4 of the ANWB *Fietsgids Zeeland*, and the signed Valkenisse route, no. 8 in the *Fietsgids*. This particular ANWB route drops down along the sea coast to Vlissingen. Here you can watch from the boulevard tiny pilot boats guiding enormous ships on the Western Scheldt towards the port of Antwerp. If you add Vlissingen to your ride you can cycle back to Middelburg via the tow path along the Kanaal door Walcheren.

I have added an extension, or a second day trip, to Delta-Expo. The first part of this extension follows the LF 1 route described in chapter 16 (Long-Distance Rides) from Middelburg to Delta-Expo, and you will see the green-on-white LF signs. At the far end of Veersegatdam in De Banjaard is a good restaurant. From here you can already see the white towers of the Eastern Scheldt barrier reaching up to the sky. The return route goes via the town of Veere over the sluices in the Kanaal van Walcheren.You'll find them marked on the ANWB map. This is a crossing for pedestrians and cyclists only.

CHAPTER 15

The Wadden Isles: Sand Dunes and Sea Air

The 5 Wadden Isles, lying in a neat curve north of the mainland, separated from the rest of the country by the Wadden Sea, are from west to east: Texel, Vlieland, Terschelling, Ameland, and Schiermonnikoog. Texel (pop. 13,000) is the largest of the 5, measuring 25 by 8 kilometers (15.5 by 5 miles), and Schiermonnikoog (pop. 1,000) is the smallest at 16 by 4 kilometers (10 by 2.5 miles).

Administratively, Texel belongs to the province of North Holland and the 4 others to the province of Friesland. I gave

Vlieland visitors board the ferryboat for the return trip to Harlingen.

the islands a chapter of their own because they are a group apart. To begin with, they are islands and the only way to reach them is by ferry boat. They're also all 5 very much alike. On the North Sea side they are lined with wide cream-colored sandy beaches which are great for walking on and for swimming. On the Wadden Sea side, when the tide is low, are mud flats you can venture on. Stay close to the coast or go with a guide if the island provides one—ask the local VVV. Within the perimeter of the shorelines are sand dunes covered with maram grass or other sand-anchoring plants, modest woods of conifers and deciduous trees, parts set aside as nature preserves and bird sanctuaries (closed during the breeding season), and occasional pastures and fields.

Each island also has an old-time lighthouse that still blinks at night, one or two villages with a baker, a butcher, and a souvenir shop, and campsites, bungalows, pensions, and hotels for the mostly Dutch visitors. Tourists come during long holiday weekends, school vacations, and in summer; at such times it may be hard to find overnight accommodations on short notice.

Special lures of the islands are the clean bracing sea air and the birds. Many birders are amazed by the variety and number

Birdwatchers on Schiermonnikoog island, hoping to add yet another bird to the many they have already spotted. (Photo Ib Huysman)

of birds that can be spotted. An address for bird-watching tours is in Appendix A.

Well-marked bikeways and footpaths crisscross the islands in orderly Dutch fashion. You'll find the islands to be almost empty of cars because visitors tend to leave them on the mainland (on Vlieland and Schiermonnikoog visitors' cars are not allowed). Rental bicycles in various sizes and models, as well as child seats, are plentiful on all the islands.

Of the 5 islands, Texel is the easiest to reach. A ferry leaves from Den Helder north of Amsterdam every hour and takes 15 minutes. The ferries for Vlieland and Terschelling leave from Harlingen in Friesland, for Ameland from Holwerd in Friesland, and for Schiermonnikoog from Lauwersoog in Groningen. The crossings are scheduled 2 or 3 times a day and take

This couple visiting Terschelling island in January have the beach to themselves.

The floor of this Vlieland restaurant is covered with sand.

at least 45 minutes. There are parking lots near the ferry terminals, which you can also reach by public transportation. Terschelling is on ANWB map no. 1, Vlieland, Terschelling, and Ameland are on map no. 2, and Schiermonnikoog is on map no. 3.

Through the years I've visited all the islands. On Vlieland we stayed at the Strandhotel, perched on a sand dune off the North Sea beach—at that time a pleasant two-star hotel that has apparently been replaced by a more elaborate establishment. We cycled to the hotel on bicycles we rented in the village near the ferry. On Schiermonnikoog we stayed one spring in ***Hotel Duinzicht, which means Dune View. Here we took the public bus from the ferry to the hotel and rented our bicycles around the corner. Some hotels on the islands have a guest- and luggage pickup service from the ferry.

I have not suggested any particular cycling routes in this chapter. Each island's VVV has maps and cycling routes and on the smaller islands it's almost impossible to get lost. If you stay more than a day you'll know all the cycling possibilities by heart. On these small island circuits you'll most likely meet the same senior couple or the same family of 4 on their bicycles or at refreshment stops several times during one day. This creates a feeling of fellowship among island guests.

Part III

Other Ways to See the Country

CHAPTER 16

Long-Distance Cycling Tours

This chapter is written for those of you who want something more challenging than cycling loop-routes that take only a few hours. Here I discuss long-distance rides, some of which may take several days.

The Stichting Landelijk Fietsplatform (National Cycling Program Foundation), an umbrella for a number of Dutch organizations involved with cycling, has recently mapped and described, in 2 guidebooks, a network of 5,500 kilometers (3,300 miles) of bicycle routes. These routes connect important cities and recreational areas and are known as the country's LF routes. (The L is taken from the word *landelijk*, which not only means rural, but also national, and the F is from *fietsroute*, bicycle route.) Selected for greatest possible cycling safety and best possible scenery, the LF's do not always take the shortest route between 2 points, but they are all connected. You can

Twenty tall, curved concrete slabs form a screen so wind can't hurl ships against the side of the Caland canal in South Holland.

cycle up and down Holland, from east to west, from west to east, or diagonally across, and never leave the LF network, signed already here and there with green-on-white shields in both directions.

The first LF to be signed and officially opened, in the spring of 1989, was the LF 1, which then went 90 kilometers into Belgium. This is the Noordzeeroute, North Sea route, that follows the North Sea coastline from Den Helder in the province of North Holland to the Belgian-French border south of Diksmuide in Belgian Flanders. Originally, the total length of the LF 1 was 360 kilometers, but in 1991 the route was continued as far as Boulogne-sur-Mer in France, adding another 90 kilometers.

If you've never been to Holland, the LF 1 will give you a nice introduction to the Dutch coastal provinces, and a sampling of Belgium to boot. The Dutch and Belgian parts of the route are shown in the LF 1 Noordzeeroute guide from north to south on 10 different pages with maps. If you also wish to use ANWB tourist maps, you will need nos. 1, 5, 6, 10, and 12, and a map of Belgian Flanders. The LF 1 is signed all the way in both directions, and some cyclists have ridden the route just

In neighboring Belgium, the LF 1 leads along a long stretch of the Damse Vaart. (Photo Titia van Rijckevorsel)

Clear LF 1 signs (green lettering on white background) mark the Noordzee route in both directions. (Photo courtesy LF)

by following the signs. If there is wind from the southwest, start the route in Belgium to avoid headwinds.

For almost all of the first 100 kilometers out of Den Helder, if you opt for the north-south direction, you cycle on bikeways far from automobiles through the coastal dunes, Holland's natural bastions against the North Sea. You also pedal through The Hague, gentlest of the Rim City cities, and the seaside resort of Scheveningen. At Maassluis you take a ferry across the Nieuwe Waterweg, the busy waterway carrying giant ships to the North Sea. Then you are on the islands of South Holland and Zeeland, where you cycle over Holland's man-made defenses against the North Sea, the dams of the Delta Plan. On the islands you traverse polderland, going from one old village to the next. You can see the church towers from afar and you might consider how in the past travelers on a horse or on foot had only those church towers to guide them, points in the landscape that promised an inn to spend the night, a place to buy bread and a tankard of beer. Today's LF cyclists can sleep in campgrounds or in youth hostels or in a variety of pensions or hotels. The LF guidebooks list pertinent addresses.

On the island of Walcheren you cycle through the town of Middelburg, which is said to have more houses, churches, and other buildings on the national monument list than any other town of similar size in Holland. You take a ferry across another waterway, the Western Scheldt, into Zeeland-Flanders and in Sluis cycle into Belgium, an undramatic entry now that custom barriers and persons who stamp passports have been abolished between The Netherlands and Belgium.

Belgian Flanders looks much the same as Zeeland-Flanders, more flat polderland with roads on dikes. For quite a

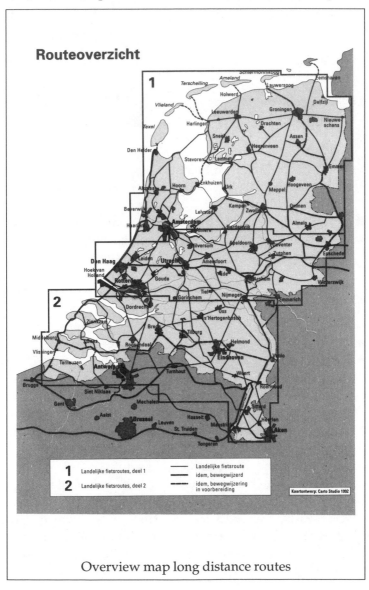

Overview map long distance routes

while you cycle on a road that once was a tow path along a canal. Both sides are lined with poplars that are reflected in the water. Then you reach Bruges (Brugge in Flemish) with hundreds of traditional-style houses along canals lined with bumpy cobblestoned streets. One of Bruges' several old squares, 't Zand, dates back to the 12th century and is being renovated with, among other things, a brand-new fountain amid groups of statues made out of steel. One such group is of 4 cyclists standing near their bicycles. A plaque quotes one of the 15th-century Medici, Il Magnifico:

> *Quant' é bella giovinezza*
> *che si fugge tuttavia*
> *di domian no v'é certezza*
> *chi vuol esser lieto sia*

> How beautiful is youth
> That flees away
> You are not certain of tomorrow
> Be joyful if you want

A message to all cyclists passing by the monument?

If you are short on time, you might end (or begin) the LF 1 in Brugge because the stretch between Brugge and the French border is much the same as the stretch between Brugge and the Dutch border. History buffs may like to visit Diksmuide, though, to see Dodengang, corridor of the dead. Here you see replicas of the trenches of the Yserfront of the First World War. Germans on one side and Belgians on the other dug themselves in, often no more than 100 meters apart, and for 4 years fought each other at a cost of many, many thousands of lives.

Unless you cycle this or any other LF on your own bicycle or you ride the LF in both directions, you're likely to need a Dutch train to transport you and your bicycle back to the point at which you rented it. This is feasible but not easy for the uninitiated. When I rode the LF 1 in 1989 with a Dutch friend from The Hague, we made 5 train changes and found the undertaking a challenge. We did eventually arrive wherever we wanted to arrive, and a place like Diksmuide in Belgium is not exactly the hub of the universe.

LF 1 Trip Notes

We cycled the LF 1 in early October on 3-speeds with hand-brakes in 6 days. It drizzled one afternoon, and rain came down steadily another morning but our rainsuits kept us dry. We traveled without reservations and stayed in the following hotels:

Bergen aan Zee: ***Meyer Hotel;

Noordwijk: ***Hotel Zeerust;

Brielle: **Atlas Hotel, with an excellent restaurant in an annex;

Middelburg: ***Hotel du Commerce.

LF Publications

As of mid-1992, the Fietsplatform organization has published four guides, for sale in Holland at ANWB offices and specialized bookstores, or order by mail from the publisher (see Appendix A), paying by money order or bank check in Dutch guilders. All have the format 15 x 21 cm (6 x 8¼) and some come in a ziplock bag with loose-leaf four-color maps. The first two include descriptions in Dutch and a Dutch-English-German glossary, so they are useful even if you don't speak the language.

Landelijke Fietsroutes deel 1 (f. 29.50)
Covers the central and northern parts of the country.

Landelijke Fietsroutes deel 2 (f. 29.50)
Covers central and southern parts of the country and adjacent Flanders in Belgium.

LF 1 Noordzee-route (f. 10.00)
Covers the route between Den Helder and the French-Belgian border. No route descriptions but maps and notes about local sights.

LF 4 Midden-Nederlandroute (f. 10.00)
Covers the 250-km route between The Hague and Enschede.

CHAPTER 17

Four-day Cycling Events

An alternative to choosing from among the routes descibed in this book is to participate in a highly structured, very Dutch four-day bicycle event, a *fietsvierdaagse,* which allows you to cycle in the company of many others. These events are scheduled from mid-May to mid-August in various parts of Holland and all draw hundreds or thousands of participants. The country's largest *fietsvierdaagse,* in the province of Drenthe, drew 31,000 riders in 1990, its 25th anniversary year.

Each of the 4 days of the *fietsvierdaagse* you start at the same point, then cycle via a different route a daily distance you register for—maybe 40, 60, or 100 kilometers—through pastures, fields, woods, and villages. Routes are indicated with a *pijl,* an arrow, or described on sheets of paper issued daily at the checking-out stand.

At the end of the fourth day you receive a medal or certificate testifying that you completed the distances you signed up for. A *fietsvierdaagse* is not a race—in fact, the organizers quite specifically discourage *hardrijden,* riding fast. These are leisurely events, and you can take as much time as you need, provided you are back before the checking-in stand closes.

To learn dates of *fietsvierdaagsen* and addresses of the organizers, write for the annual publication of the Nederlandse Toer Fiets Unie (NTFU), or Netherlands Tour Cycling Union (see Appendix A). The text of this pamphlet is in Dutch only. Enclose international postal reply coupons to receive the pamphlet by airmail. In 1992 it listed 24 *fietsvierdaagsen,* as well as 3 three-day events and 2 two-day events. A Netherlands Board of Tourism office near your home may have NTFU schedules in stock.

If the idea of joining the Dutch on bicycles in such a four-day stint appeals to you, pick one or two events from the NTFU listing that suit your travel dates and write the organizer for details. Allow plenty of time for a reply. Most members of the organizational staffs are volunteers who also have other commitments. Most organizers can provide translations of the route directions and otherwise assist non-Dutch speakers if you ask them far enough ahead of time.

Participants in the Fietsvierdaagsen are of all ages and ride all kinds of bicycles: standard bicycles without gears and with a coaster brake, three-speeds with handbrakes, mountain bikes, racing bicycles, and models in between.

CHAPTER 18

Day Programs
with the Railroads

Another way to tour Holland is on the package trips offered by NS, the Dutch Railroads. The small size of Holland permits you to take an early train at almost any NS station to almost any other NS station, make a city tour on foot, walk or cycle in the countryside, or visit an attraction, and arrive back at your hotel before midnight, all at a package price.

Information and prices on package outings are published in an annual booklet, titled in 1991 *Er-Op-Uit!* (let's go!) for sale at NS ticket counters. It had 256 pages and listed 72 day trips to attractions like zoos, amusement parks, museums (in the *NS-Dagtochten* section), 47 bicycle rides (in the *ANWB-Fiets-tochten* section), 33 walks (in the *SLAW-Wandelingen* section), and 44 city walks (in the *VVV-Stadswandelingen* section).

At your train departure station tell the ticket clerk which outing you wish to make. You will then receive a roundtrip

Cyclists on a NS day trip out of Castricum parked their rented bikes to walk to the North Sea beach.

train ticket, voucher for entrance fees, if applicable, and perhaps voucher for a cup of coffee and pie en route. You may pay up to 30 percent less than if you buy the elements separately. The walking routes often lead you to a station other than the one you started from.

The text in the NS booklet is entirely in Dutch, but you will be able to extract useful information just by looking at the photographs, sketch maps, and lists. The *VVV-Stadswandelingen* section, for example, contains a list of the names and telephone numbers of VVV's in more than 40 cities that have mapped and described city walks of 3 to 6 kilometers length. The VVV, which is often located near the station, will have documentation in English available at a nominal cost, and for 19 of these city walks you can rent a walkman with a cassette tape in English. Rental is 5 guilders a day, and the VVV asks for a deposit of 50 to 150 guilders, or you can leave an I.D. or a Euro-check or travelers check with the VVV instead.

The *Fietstochten* section has a list of *Fietsverhuurbedrijven* (bicycle rental shops) at or near the station at which you can rent a bicycle at a reduced fee. Get the bicycle rental ticket at the NS ticket counter upon showing your train ticket. You'll also receive a route description to lead you along a route marked with ANWB's hexagonal red-on-white or green-on-white loop-route signs. The routes are from 20 to 60 kilometers.

The walks listed in the *SLAW-Wandelingen* section are organized in the same manner: upon arrival at the station where your walk starts you buy your route map. You'll be following a route set out and signed by the long-distance walk organization SLAW, discussed in chapter 22. The routes range from 10 to 18 kilometers and are marked with red and white stripes.

A caveat regarding NS outings: Walkmen for city walks may be in short supply and rental bicycles go quickly, particularly in summer. Reserve yours by phone as early as you can. Not all of the bicycle rental places that are part of the NS programs rent three-speeds with handbrakes. If that's what you want, you may have to make a few more phone calls and settle for another NS bicycle trip. The list in Appendix B may be of help.

CHAPTER 19

Multiday VVV Cycling Arrangements

Perhaps you would like to cycle through Holland for a few days, but don't want to be bothered organizing it yourself—renting the bicycle, reserving the hotel, getting the right maps, figuring out the routes. And neither do you want to join an escorted group tour where all these things are done for you. VVV visitor bureaus may have the answer: one of the *fietsarrangementen*, cycling arrangements, that they put together and market.

These programs are for 3 to 10 days and may be started any day (in season), or only certain days of the week. When you arrive at the starting point of the program you have selected, you receive an ANWB or other map as well as detailed route descriptions and sightseeing tips, in English when available. The organizing VVV has reserved a bicycle for you at a bicycle rental place (specify ahead if you want a 3-speed with hand-

The 17-km Markerwaarddijk between Enkhuizen and Lelystad is part of a cross-country tour organized by VVV Gelderland.

brakes). The bicycle has side panniers to carry your personal belongings, or the VVV will provide an (often free) *koffernabrengservice*, luggage transport service, between hotels.

As confirmed in vouchers you receive ahead of time, the VVV has already booked your rooms. They either have private amenities or a bathroom and toilet down the hall. Some programs let you stay 2 or even 3 nights in one hotel so you don't have to pack and unpack every day. All programs end where they start.

The price, which you pay in advance, usually includes bicycle rental, documentation, hotel, and breakfast and dinner in hotel. Supplements for single occupancy of a room apply. The total price tends to be much lower than of an escorted cycling tour because with a VVV arrangement you don't pay for a tour escort's salary nor towards group tour services such as a support van.

By 1991, the following VVV's had *fietsarrangement* information and route descriptions for some of their tours available in English. I'm listing the VVV's here by province; in parentheses is one sample tour of each VVV to show the variety in the combined programs. Addresses of the organizing can be found in Appendix A.

This sign marks a wheelchair-accessible fishing spot near Alkmaar.

Drenthe: provincial VVV
Eight-day tour of Drenthe, Holland's prime cycling province, 40–50 km a day.

Friesland: provincial VVV
Seven-day 11-town tour following the 230-km ANWB-signed route, 40–45 km a day.

Gelderland: provincial VVV
Six-day tour taking you to 3 different sections of Gelderland, 40–65 km a day.

Limburg: provincial VVV
Seven-day tour with hilly rides, crossing the Dutch borders into Belgium and Germany, 30–60 km a day.

North Brabant: VVV Parkland Brabant
Five-day tour for culinary experts, 40 km a day.

North Holland: VVV Gooi & Vechtstreek
Seven-day tour around Lake IJssel, 380 km, can be shortened by omitting the 32-km enclosing dam and taking a boat from Enkhuizen to Stavoren instead, 55-60 km a day.

Overijssel: provincial VVV
Six-day tour through Twente area, 45 km a day.

Cyclists in Het Gooi region pass by fluitekruit (althryscus sylvestris) that flowers from April to August. (Photo couretesy VVV Noord Holland)

South Holland: VVV Dordrecht

Nine-day tour of old Dutch towns with two-night stays in each one; includes Kinderdijk windmills; daily cycling distance up to you.

Zeeland: provincial VVV

This VVV was just starting cycling arrangements, some geared to English-speaking tourists.

Many VVV cycling packages are listed in the annual *Holland Cycling* brochure available at a Netherlands Board of Tourism office in your country or at VVV's in Holland. This brochure also lists tour operators based in the United States and Canada who offer escorted group tours in Holland.

All VVV cycling arrangements are best reserved well ahead of time, especially if you plan to go during the tourist season. Correspond or telephone direct with the VVV. From year to year the selection of arrangements may differ as programs are dropped or new ones are added.

CHAPTER 20

Covered Wagon Touring

A whimsical variation on the VVV arrangements discussed in the previous chapter are 3- to 5-day VVV *huifkararrangementen* (covered wagon tours). So far these are offered only by the VVV's Eindhoven and Kempenland in North Brabant and by VVV Drenthe.

In Drenthe you bring your own sleeping bag to sleep on a mattress in the wagon and prepare meals yourself. You can decide how far to travel each day. In North Brabant you sleep in country hotels, eat breakfast and dinner in the hotel, and receive a packed lunch. Folding table and chairs and picnic supplies come with the wagon. Daily distances average 20

Two youngsters drive their covered touring wagon near Waalre in North Brabant.

It is the tourists' responsibility to harness the pony for another day.

kilometers. For both types of tours you receive route descriptions and instructions on how to harness and unharness the pony. The literature is available in English.

Book these arrangements through the organizing VVV. If you want to rent a covered wagon just for a day to go clippity-clopping through the countryside, you can write or phone the Van Och family directly. They are based in Waalre in North Brabant. Or you may just want to stop at the Van Ochs' restaurant to sit at one of the inevitable white outdoor tables on a white chair and drink *Trappist van 't vat*, Trappist [beer] from the barrel, as advertised on a sign. Mrs. Van Och makes *Kempische pannekoek*, Kempen pancake, 30 centimeters in diameter. This is an old Brabant recipe that features mushrooms, bacon, sausage, ham, spices, and onions.

CHAPTER 21

Cruising the Waterways

A very special way to tour Holland is in a rented boat on the inland waterways. You have your choice among the big rivers of the Rhine and Meuse and their tributaries, little streams, canals, old lakes, new lakes like the *randmeren* (border lakes) in Flevoland, the closed-off sea arms in Zeeland, or a combination thereof, a total of nearly 6,000 kilometers or 3,600 miles of navigable waters. You also have your choice of craft for such an undertaking: canoe, open sailboat, cabin yacht with sails and (auxiliary) motor, cabin yacht with only a motor, or a traditional brown ship, so called because of her brown sails, although some have white ones. In the past, a *tjalk* (spritsail barge), *klipper* (clipper), *schoener* (schooner), and other such ships plied the inland waterways and sometimes the seas beyond, carrying cargo in their holds. Now the holds have been remodeled with berths, showers, and other amenities to please visitors while a skipper and sometimes a crew sail the ship.

Dutch high school students on a field trip tackle the unfurling of the main sail of a chartered clipper.

In your boat or canoe you glide past meadows and fields, through villages and ancient little towns where you can go ashore. On the water, you'll be sure to see Dutch out in their own boats. The people of Holland own more pleasure boats per capita than inhabitants of any other country in the world. Perhaps you'll get to meet some of these boat-owning Dutch as your boats lie tied up next to each other in a yacht harbor or wait to go through a lock together (very few locks in Holland are self-operable as they often are in France), or wait for a bridge to open. In Holland, commercial traffic on water has priority over road traffic. If you have already driven a car or ridden a bicycle in Holland, you may have had to wait in a long line for a bridge to slowly go up and then slowly go down so a barge or a string of pleasure boats could proceed on their way.

Your choice of rental craft will depend on the kind of waterways you wish to travel—dead water, water with currents, or open water—, on your expertise with a craft, on your budget, and on your physical fitness.

Paddling a canoe is hard work, whether it's a kayak for 1 or 2 persons using two-bladed paddles, or a *Canadees*, a Canadian, with Eskimo-style one-bladed paddles.

A rented houseboat takes a family through one of the little canals in Hindeloopen, Friesland. (Photo courtesy Nickel Rijk)

On some canoe routes you have to pass a weir, *stuw* in Dutch, and if it isn't safe to paddle over such a dam, which it usually isn't, you must porter the canoe. Avoid rivers and canals with commercial traffic. A giant tanker or a long barge can easily miss seeing you in a canoe and also create big waves. You can rent a canoe for an hour, a day, or several days, in which case you can stow a small tent in your Canadian or kayak and sleep at a campsite or stay overnight in a hotel. Some rental canoes are made unsinkable by foam sections and air bags.

VVV's in every province can advise you on canoeing possibilities. Several issue canoeists' maps and booklets in English, such as *Groningen—850 kilometers of canoeing enjoyment.* Groningen is a good choice if you seek quiet and uncluttered waterways. For joviality and merriment with other watersport enthusiasts gathering at day's end, canoeing near the lakes of Friesland, Utrecht, or South Holland is a better bet. The lakes themselves, however, are likely to be windy and crowded with all kinds of sailboats.

To be one of those sailors, you can usually rent a small open boat called BM or a $16m^2$, a *zestienskwadraat* (meaning 16 square meters of sail), in any sailing area of Holland. These

Lock in the river Linde, in Overijssel, is filling up with pleasurecraft.

boats are 6 meters long. You can rent them by the hour or the day and rent a deck tent to enable you to sleep aboard.

For grander overnight accommodations aboard, rent a cabin yacht with sails and an (auxiliary) motor or a cabin yacht with only a motor. The latter are available in all sizes and degrees of comfort and are popular with foreign tourists who have no sailing expertise. Larger cabin yachts can also go on Lake IJssel and the Wadden Sea, but be advised that Lake IJssel can act like the rambunctious sea it once was. The Wadden Sea has tricky low tides when, except for a few navigable gulleys, the sea falls dry.

As of April 1992 a law is in effect in Holland requiring all sailors of boats longer than 15 meters, or able to go more than 20 kilometers per hour, to have a *vaarbewijs* (sailing license). How this affects foreign visitors was not known at the time of writing this book.

A sailing license is not required for a motorboat especially designed by Friesland Boating in Koudum for touring shallow waters in Friesland and Groningen. Although I am not mechanically adept, I found one of these boats easy to handle. It has space for bicycles, sleeps from 4 to 8 persons, and would be attractive for a low-key, slow-paced family outing on a level with the covered wagons in North Brabant. During the summer the minimal rental period is one week.

All rental boats, except canoes and small open boats, must have water traffic regulations on board. These differ for the Rhine, other inland waterways, some Zeeland waters, and the sea (an area beyond the scope of this book). You'll find the traffic rules, in Dutch, in the Royal Dutch Touring Club ANWB's *Almanak voor Watertoerisme, Deel I*. Any medium-sized rental firm will have some traffic rules written up in English.

If you don't care to familiarize yourself with water traffic rules, read charts, and figure out your route, yet yearn to make a sailing voyage and don't know a jib from a mainsail, consider chartering one of the skippered brown ships for a weekend or a week. A day trip may also be possible. The brown ships carry from 6 to 36 passengers overnight (more during the day). Some ships are graded with stars, just as hotels are. Some are *plat-*

bodems, with flat bottoms and leeboards on the sides. You can help with the sailing or let yourself be sailed, do your own cooking or enjoy catered meals. The ships sail on the larger canals and rivers, but also on Lake IJssel and the Wadden Sea. Ships are often permitted to rest on a tidal flat at ebb so you can step down on the sand and walk on the bottom of the Wadden Sea. The basic charter price of the higher priced traditionals may shock you (3,400 guilders for a weekend in a five-star clipper with 28 beds), but if several families or members of a group chip in, the per-person cost per day is less than a room in a five-star hotel.

Offices of the Netherlands Board of Tourism abroad have an annual folder on boating in Holland and the booklets *Canoeing in Holland*, *Boat Rental*, *Traditional Sailing*, and (Wind) *Surfing and Sailing Schools*. They all give rental addresses, and rental prices except for the canoes.

Barges being let through at a lock in the Lek canal in Utrecht province.

In Holland the VVV visitor bureaus will also have most of these brochures. The ANWB *Almanak, Deel II* (available at ANWB offices, VVV's, and most watersports shops in Holland) is almost 750 pages of information about all navigable waterways in Holland. It covers such subjects as speed limits on the water, operation of bridges and locks (some close on Sundays), moorings, launderettes, and chemical and refuse disposal. The text is in Dutch, but 7 pages in English tell you how to use the *Almanak* and explain the various subjects covered in it.

The annual ANWB *Nederland vaarkaart* (cruising map), scale 1 : 500,000, is only available at ANWB offices. It shows waterways differently colored according to the maximum height of ships admissable, the height being determined by the lowest fixed bridge on the route. For actual navigation you will need to buy sectional ANWB *waterkaarten*, scale 1 : 10,000, at ANWB offices (if you are a member of an affilliated organization) or in specialized bookstores. L.J. Harri, near the central railroad station in Amsterdam, sells nautical maps for areas around the world.

CHAPTER 22

Excursions on Foot

This last chapter tells you about a way of exploring Holland's backroads that might be considered the most natural and intimate way: on foot. You can reach areas not even accessible by bicycle.

For walking you have the same options as mentioned for cycling: long-distance, four-day event, VVV arrangement, train package, or an excursion of a few hours or a day that you entirely plan yourself. Stichting Lange-Afstand Wandelpaden (SLAW, or Foundation of Long-distance Foot Paths) publishes helpful maps and guidebooks. The guiding material is all in Dutch but the SLAW *Nederland* map that shows where the routes are has a summary of the map's text in English. Buy SLAW publications from SLAW, in specialized bookstores, or at VVV's.

By 1990 SLAW had mapped and marked, with the help of volunteers, a 3,500-kilometer "harmonious network of connecting walking routes through Holland's green spaces" as formulated in the foundation's bylaws. Blocks with a painted white stripe above a painted red stripe—the block about 10 centimeters wide and high—mark the SLAW routes. Two white and red blocks stacked on top of one another mean "Careful, a change in direction is coming up." A white line and a red line that form an X means "You are wrong, this is not the route."

Here are some routes, with details translated from the SLAW Nederland map. LAW 1-1, *Zevenwoudenpad* (Seven Forests Path), runs from Lauwersoog in Groningen to Uffelte in Drenthe. The one-way distance is 150 kilometers. "This path through eastern Friesland shows an unexpected part of this water province (…) *coulissen* landscape (fields dressed up with trees)." The 7 forests are not the kind that blow you over by their vastness or majestic grandeur, but it is pleasant to be under trees for part of your walk.

LAW 5-5, *Wad-en Wierdenpad* (Tidal Flat and Mounds Path), goes from Lauwersoog to Nieuweschans, both in Groningen. One-way distance is 120 kilometers. "Along the tidal flats and through the countryside of Groningen, over little bridges, past pools, rivulets, and historic moat-girded farms with beautifully laid-out gardens."

LAW 5-2, *Visserspad* (Fishermen's Path), runs from Hook of Holland to The Hague and Haarlem. The distance is 105 kilometers "through Holland's unexpectedly quiet and lovely sand dunes, under the smoke of Rim City."

The longest named walk is the 464-kilometer *Pieterpad* from Pieterburen in the province of Groningen to the St. Pietersberg, a 110-meter-high mountain in the province of Limburg. The path came about thanks to Toos Goorhuis from Tilburg in North Brabant and Bertje Jens from the city of Groningen who thought it would be fun to have a walking route from the northern tip of the country to the very south. So the 2 women studied topographical maps, planned routes, and tried them out, sometimes 3 different versions. It took 4 years of walking weekends and vacation days to outline the route and gather the data for the route descriptions now printed up in 2 guides. Each year thousands of people walk at least a section of the *Pieterpad*, either one day at a time, returning home in the evening, or in several consecutive days. Some hotels along the route bear a sign "Pieterpad walkers are welcome here." The path connects with the *grandes randonnées*, long-distance walking routes, of Western Europe.

There's only one 4-day walking event of note. It takes place the second half of July in and around the town of Nijmegen in the province of Gelderland and is called *De Vierdaagse*, The Four Days. It is organized by the KNBLO (Royal Netherlands League for Physical Culture). As with the 4-day cycling events, you walk a different route of the length for which you registered each day. The minimum daily distance is 30 kilometers (18 miles), the maximum is 50 kilometers (30 miles). In 1991 *De Vierdaagse* celebrated its 75th birthday; almost 39,000 walkers from 43 countries started off and 35,475 completed the 4 days. All *Vierdaagse* material is available in English as well as in German and French.

Patterned after the VVV *fietsarrangementen*, cycling arrangements, whereby you cycle from hotel to hotel and your luggage may be transported for you, are VVV *wandelarrangementen*, walking arrangements. Not as many are on the market as there are for cycling, and hardly any are geared to the English-speaking tourist. At the time of writing, only the VVV Limburg offered a 3-day walking tour between hotels, including luggage courier service, with route descriptions in English.

As already mentioned in chapter 18, the day outings of the Netherlands railroads in the 1991 NS booklet *Er-Op-Uit!* included 33 walks you can make in combination with a train from any NS station in The Netherlands. The walks from 10 to 18 kilometers are all marked with the white and red stripes of the SLAW foundation, and are often part of a long-distance path. NS route pamphlets, which you can buy at the station from which your walk starts, all feature a map section with the route superimposed in a different color, probably enough to guide you even if you can't read a word of the copious Dutch

Hikers are alone as they walk along a Wiericke canal on a walk mapped and signed by South Holland province. (Photo Ivo van Rijckevorsel)

text. The 1991 pamphlets were entitled *Natuurwandelingen van station naar station*, Nature Walks from Station to Station. You usually end your walk at a different NS station than the one at which you began.

You may want something even less structured than an NS walk and you'll find that Holland has plenty of footpaths and walking routes from which to choose. Many routes have been described in booklets and pamphlets; they are usually only in Dutch, but if they have a clear map section or detailed sketch map you may have enough information to walk by. Where to go? Stop at a VVV and ask for walking suggestions or look at an ANWB tourist map for walking areas near where you're staying. These are indicated by a symbol, and sometimes the footpaths themselves are marked by brown broken lines. You'll always find footpaths in nature preserves or in the country's national parks (pink or green on the map). Every national park has a walking map for sale at the entrance. Some of the country's national parks are small, at least by American standards, so if your prime motive is to make a good brisk walk of several hours, inquire whether a particular park is for you.

New footpaths and walking routes are regularly opened here and there with official ceremonies and reported on in the press. The province of South Holland, for example, has just published a series of pamphlets on walks that average 20 kilometers in strictly rural areas. It's part of the province's Green Heart of Holland promotion (see South Holland chapter). The new routes are marked with colorful posts and use, where possible, paths left in their natural state. "Wear sturdy shoes," advise the pamphlets. These pamphlets are available from VVV's in the walk area or from the province; see address in Appendix A.

You'll notice that walking routes in The Netherlands often take you through the same areas as the cycling routes do—through the country's precious green spaces where, in a world of noise and chaos, you can still find calm and peace.

Appendix

Verklaring

Schaal 1:100.000

(1cm op de kaart is 1 km in het terrein)

0 1 2 3 4 5 km

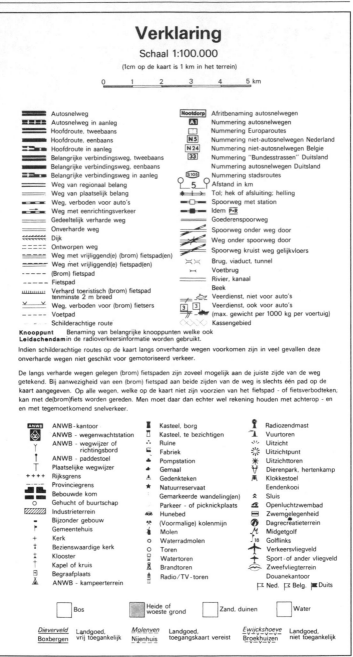

Autosnelweg	**Nootdorp**	Afritbenaming autosnelwegen
Autosnelweg in aanleg	**A1**	Nummering autosnelwegen
Hoofdroute, tweebaans		Nummering Europaroutes
Hoofdroute, eenbaans	**N5**	Nummering niet-autosnelwegen Nederland
Hoofdroute in aanleg	**N24**	Nummering niet-autosnelwegen Belgie
Belangrijke verbindingsweg, tweebaans	**33**	Nummering "Bundesstrassen" Duitsland
Belangrijke verbindingsweg, eenbaans		Nummering autosnelwegen Duitsland
Belangrijke verbindingsweg in aanleg	**S105**	Nummering stadsroutes
Weg van regionaal belang	5	Afstand in km
Weg van plaatselijk belang		Tol; hek of afsluiting; helling
Weg, verboden voor auto's		Spoorweg met station
Weg met eenrichtingsverkeer	**P·R**	Idem
Gedeeltelijk verharde weg		Goederenspoorweg
Onverharde weg		Spoorweg onder weg door
Dijk		Weg onder spoorweg door
Ontworpen weg		Spoorweg kruist weg gelijkvloers
Weg met vrijliggend(e) (brom) fietspad(en)		Brug, viaduct, tunnel
Weg met vrijliggend(e) fietspad(en)		Voetbrug
(Brom) fietspad		Rivier, kanaal
Fietspad		Beek
Verhard toeristisch (brom) fietspad tenminste 2 m breed		Veerdienst, niet voor auto's
Weg, verboden voor (brom) fietsers	**3** **3**	Veerdienst, ook voor auto's (max. gewicht per 1000 kg per voertuig)
Voetpad		Kassengebied
Schilderachtige route		

Knooppunt Benaming van belangrijke knooppunten welke ook
Leidschendam in de radioverkeersinformatie worden gebruikt.

Indien schilderachtige routes op de kaart langs onverharde wegen voorkomen zijn in veel gevallen deze
onverharde wegen niet geschikt voor gemotoriseerd verkeer.

De langs verharde wegen gelegen (brom) fietspaden zijn zoveel mogelijk aan de juiste zijde van de weg
getekend. Bij aanwezigheid van een (brom) fietspad aan beide zijden van de weg is slechts één pad op de
kaart aangegeven. Op alle wegen, welke op de kaart niet zijn voorzien van het fietspad - of fietsverbodteken,
kan met de(brom)fiets worden gereden. Men moet daar dan echter wel rekening houden met achterop - en
en met tegemoetkomend snelverkeer.

ANWB ANWB-kantoor	Kasteel, borg	Radiozendmast
ANWB - wegenwachtstation	Kasteel, te bezichtigen	Vuurtoren
ANWB - wegwijzer of richtingsbord	Ruine	Uitzicht
ANWB - paddestoel	Fabriek	Uitzichtpunt
Plaatselijke wegwijzer	Pompstation	Uitzichttoren
Rijksgrens	Gemaal	Dierenpark, hertenkamp
Provinciegrens	Gedenkteken	Klokkestoel
Bebouwde kom	Natuurreservaat	Eendenkooi
Gehucht of buurtschap	Gemarkeerde wandeling(en)	Sluis
Industrieterrein	Parkeer - of picknickplaats	Openluchtzwembad
Bijzonder gebouw	Hunebed	Zwemgelegenheid
Gemeentehuis	(Voormalige) kolenmijn	Dagrecreatieterrein
Kerk	Molen	Midgetgolf
Bezienswaardige kerk	Waterradmolen	Golflinks
Klooster	Toren	Verkeersvliegveld
Kapel of kruis	Watertoren	Sport - of ander vliegveld
Begraafplaats	Brandtoren	Zweefvliegterrein
ANWB - kampeerterrein	Radio/TV - toren	Douanekantoor
		Ned. Belg. Duits

Bos	Heide of woeste grond	Zand, duinen	Water

Dieverveld Landgoed, vrij toegankelijk
Boxbergen

Molenven Landgoed, toegangskaart vereist
Nijenhuis

Ewijckshoeve Landgoed, niet toegankelijk
Broekhuizen

ANWB map legend

Note: for English translation of legend terms, see page 214

Addresses of Organizations, Sights, and Hotels

For general information outside Holland:

Australia: Netherlands Board of Tourism (NBT), 5 Elizabeth Street, 6th Floor, Sydney NSW 2000. Tel. 02-2476921.

Canada: Netherlands Board of Tourism (NBT), 25 Adelaide Street East, Suite 710, Toronto, Ont. M5C 1Y2. Tel. (416) 363-1577.

Great Britain and Ireland: Netherlands Board of Tourism (NBT), 25-28 Buckingham Gate, London SWIE 6LD. Tel. (071) 630-0451.

U.S.A.: Netherlands Board of Tourism (NBT), 355 Lexington Avenue, 21st Floor, New York, NY 10017. Tel. (212) 370-7367.

Netherlands Board of Tourism (NBT), 225 N. Michigan Avenue, Suite 326, Chicago, IL 60601. Tel. (312) 819-0300.

For general information in Holland:

ANWB Royal Dutch Touring Club, Wassenaarseweg 220, P.O. Box 93200, 2509 BA The Hague. Tel. 070-3147147 (only for members of an affiliated auto club)

For maps:

Geografische Boekhandel Jacob van Wijngaarden, Overtoom 136, 1054 HN Amsterdam. Tel. 020-6121901.

Pied à Terre, Singel 393, 1012 WN Amsterdam. Tel. 020-6274455.

Stap voor Stap, Nieuwstad 26, 6811 BL Arnhem. Tel. 085-510334.

De Wandelwinkel, Bergkerkplein 5, 7411 EN Deventer. Tel. 05700-15077.

Verwijs, afd. reisboekhandel, Buitenhof 51, 2513 AH The Hague. Tel. 070-3639718.

De Zwerver, Oude Kijk in 't Jatstr. 43, 9712 EC Groningen. Tel. 050-126950.

Stap voor STap, v. Welderenstraat 52, 6511 MN Nijmegen. Tel. 080-234957.

Interglobe, Vinkenburgstr. 7, 3512 AA Utrecht. Tel. 030-340401.

Fietsvakantiewinkel, Spoorlaan 17, 3445 AE Woerden. Tel. 03480-21844.

For hotel reservations:

The Netherlands Reservation Centre, Postbus 404, 2260 AK Leidschendam. Tel. 070-3202500, Fax 070-3202611.

VVV Accommodation Service at any VVV office (you must visit in person; information is not given by telephone).

For specific information:
Drenthe

Provincial VVV: Postbus 10012, 9400 CA Assen. Tel. 05920-51777. (For correspondence and phone information.)

Museums and sights:

Drents Museum, Brink 1-5, Assen. Tel. 05920-12741.
't Flint'nhoes, Bronnegerstraat 12, Borger. Tel. 05998-36374.

Memorial Center Kamp Westerbork, Oosthalen 8, Hooghalen. Tel. 05939-2600.

Museum van Papierknipkunst, Hoofdstraat 16, Westerbork. Tel. 05933-31381.

Noorder Dierenpark, Hoofdstraat 18, Emmen. Tel. 05910-18800.

Zeemuseum Miramar, Vledder-
weg 25, Vledder. Tel. 05212-
1300.

Hotels:

Assen, ***Hotel de Jonge,
Brinkstraat 85, 9401 HZ Assen.
Tel. 05920-12023.

Borger, ***Hotel Bieze,
Hoofdstraat 21, 9531 AA
Borger. Tel. 05998-34321.

Dwingeloo, ***Hotel Wesseling,
Brink 26, 7991 CH Dwingeloo.
Tel. 05219-1544.

Flevoland

Provincial VVV: Postbus 548,
8200 AM Lelystad. Tel. 03200-
30500. (For correspondence and
phone information.)

Museums and sights:

Museum voor Scheepsar-
cheologie, Vossemeerdijk 21,
8251 PM Ketelhaven-Dronten.
Tel. 03210-13287.

Natuurpark Lelystad
(Meerkoetenweg). Tel. 03200-
53643/51546.

Coöperatie Nautilus, Postbus
501, 8200 AM Lelystad. Tel.
03200-80108.

Info-centrum Nieuw Land,
Oostvaardersdijk 01-13, Lelystad. Tel. 03200-60799.

Orchideeënhoeve, Ooster-
ringweg 34, Luttelgeest. Tel.
05273-2875.

Hotel:

Lelystad, ****Hotel Lelystad,
Agoraweg 11, 8224 BZ. Tel.
03200-42444.

Friesland

Provincial VVV: Stationsplein 1,
8911 AC Leeuwarden. Tel. 058-
13 22 24. (For correspondence
and phone information.)

Museums and sights:

Popta Castle, Marssum. Tel.
05107-1231, guided tours only.

Ceramic Museum Het Princes-
sehof, Grote Kerkstraat 11,
Leeuwarden, Tel. 05100-27438.

Hotel:

Koudum, ****Hotel Galamadammen, Galamadammen 1-4, 8723
CE. Tel. 05142-1346.

Gelderland

Provincial VVV: Postbus 142,
6860 AC Oosterbeek. Tel. 085-
332033. (For correspondence
and phone information.)

Museums and sights:

Airborne Museum,
Utrechtseweg 232, Oosterbeek.
Tel. 085-337710.

Kröller-Müller Museum,
Nationaal Park De Hoge
Veluwe. Tel. 08382-241.

Loevestein Castle, Brakel. Tel.
01832-1375.

Openluchtmuseum,
Schelmseweg 89, Arnhem. Tel.
085-576111.

Palace Het Loo, Koninklijk Park
1, Apeldoorn. Tel. 055-212244.

Hotels:

Arnhem, ****Rijnhotel, Onder-
langs 10, 6812 CG. Tel. 085-
434642.

Vorden, ***Hotel Bakker,
Dorpsstraat 24, 7251 BB. Tel.
05752-1312.

Wolfheze, ****De
Buunderkamp, Buunderkamp
8, 6874 NC. Tel. 08308-21166.

Restaurants:

Doorwerth Castle, Fonteinallee
4, Doorwerth. Tel. 085-333420.

Groningen

Provincial VVV: Naberpassage
3, 9712 JV, Groningen. Tel. 050-
139700. (For correspondence
and phone information.)

Museums and sights:

Flower Auction Eelde, Bur-
gemeester J.G. Legroweg 80,
Eelde. Tel. 05907-97777.

Menkemaborg, Menkemaweg 2,
Uithuizen. Tel. 05953-1970.

Old Groningen Churches Foundation, Westersingel 43, 9718 CD Groningen. Tel. 050-123569.

Hotels:

Paterswolde, *****Familiehotel, Groningerweg 19, 9765 TA Paterswolde. Tel. 05907-95400.

Sellingen, ***Hotel Homan, Dorpsstraat 8, 9551 AE Sellingen. Tel. 05992-2206.

Limburg

Provincial VVV: Postbus 811, 6300 AV Valkenburg a/d Geul. Tel. 04406-13993. (For correspondence and phone information.)

Museums and sights:

Bonnefantenmuseum, Dominikanerplein 5, Maastricht. Tel. 043-251655.

Thermae 2000, Cauberg 27, 6301 BT Valkenburg a/d Geul. Tel. 04406-16060.

Thermenmuseum, Coriovallumstraat 9, Heerlen. Tel. 045-764581.

Treasury of St. Servatius Church, Keizer Karelplein 6, Maastricht. Tel. 043-10490.

Hotels:

Kerkrade, ***Castle Erenstein, Oud Erensteinerweg 6, 6468 PC Kerkrade. Tel. 045-461333.

Landgraaf, ***Winselerhof, Tunnelweg 99, 6372 XH Landgraaf. Tel. 045-464343.

Maastricht, ***Hotel Bergère, Stationsstraat 40, 6221 BR Maastricht. Tel. 043-251651.

Maastricht, ****Hotel de l'Empereur, Stationsstraat 2, 6221 BP Maastricht. Tel. 043-213838.

Margraten, ***Hotel-Café Wippelsdaal, Groot Welsden 13, 6269 ET Margraten. Tel. 04458-1891.

Mechelen, **Hotel Hoeve de Plei, Overgeul l, 6281 BG Mechelen. Tel. 04455-1294.

Thorn, **Hotel Crasborn, Hoogstraat 6, 6017 AR Thorn. Tel. 04756-1281.

Thorn, ***Hostellerie La Ville Blanche, Hoogstraat 2, 6017 AR Thorn. Tel. 04756-2341.

Weert, ****Hotel Jan Van Der Croon, Driesveldlaan 99, 600l KC Weert. Tel. 04950-39655.

Wittem, ***Castle Wittem, Wittemerallee 3, 6286 AA Wittem. Tel. 04450-1208.

North Brabant

Provincial VVV: Postbus 3259, 5003 DG Tilburg. Tel. 013-434060. (For correspondence and phone information.)

VVV Parkland Brabant, Postbus 3259, 5003 DG Tilburg. Tel. 013-361515.

Museums and sights:

Dutch National Carillon Museum, Ostaderstraat 23, Asten. Tel. 04936-91865.

Klompenmuseum De Platijn, Broekdijk 16, Best. Tel. 04998-71247.

Van Gogh Documentation Center, Papenvoort 15, Nuenen. Tel. 040-631668.

Hotels:

's Hertogenbosch (Den Bosch), *Hotel Terminus, Stationsplein 19, 5211 AP 's Hertogenbosch. Tel. 073-130666.

North Holland

Provincial VVV: Florapark 6, 2012 HK Haarlem. Tel. 023-319413. (For correspondence and phone information.)

VVV Gooi en Vechtstreek, Adr. Dortsmanplein 1B, 1411 RC Naarden. Tel. 02159-44114.

Museums and sights:

Hans Brinker Museum, Voordam 6, Alkmaar. Tel. 072-111217.

Museum Mill, Noordervaart 2, Schermerhorn. Tel. 02202-1519.

Nic Jonk Sculpture Garden, Haviksdijkje 5, Grootschermer. Tel. 02997-1560.

Zuiderzeemuseum, Wierdijk 18, Enkhuizen. Tel. 02280-10122.

Hotels:

Amsterdam, ***Hotel Ambassade, Herengracht 341, 1016 AZ. Tel. 020-6262333. Serves only breakfast (table service).

Restaurants:

IJmuiden, Visrestaurant Kop van de Haven, Sluisplein 80. Tel. 02550-34818.

Overijssel

Provincial VVV: Het Kolkje 4, Postbus 500, 7600 AM Almelo. Tel. 05490-18767. (For correspondence and phone information.)

Museums and sights:

Arboretum Poort-Bulten, Lossersestraat, De Lutte. Tel. 05419-2005.

Huis Singraven, Molendijk 39, Denekamp. Tel. 05413-1372. (Buy tickets at restaurant De Watermolen next to waterwheel mill opposite the mansion.)

Museumboerderij Staphorst, Muldersweg 4, Staphorst. Tel. 05225-1087/1228.

Hotels:

De Lutte, ***Hotel De Lutt, Beuningerstraat 20, 7587 LD. Tel. 05415-52525.

Steenwijk, ***Hotel De Gouden Engel, Tukseweg 1-3, 8331 KZ. Tel. 05210-12436.

South Holland

Provincial VVV: 2611 GS Delft. Tel. 015-126100. (For correspondence and phone information.)

VVV Dordrecht, Stationsweg 1, 3311 JW Dordrecht. Tel. 078-132800.

Voorlichting en Inspraak van de provincie Zuid-Holland, Koningskade 1, 2596 AA The Hague. Tel. 070-116622.

Vrienden Van de Voetveren, Ringdijk 432, Ridderkerk. Tel. 01804-13304

Hotels:

Bergambacht, ****De Arendshoeve, Molenlaan 14, 2861 LB. Tel. 01825-1000.

Restaurants:

Vlaardingen, ****Delta Hotel Restaurant, Maasboulevard 15, 3133 AK. Tel. 010-4345477.

Utrecht

Provincial VVV: Europalaan 93, 3526 KP Utrecht. Tel. 030-801100. (For correspondence and phone information.)

Museums and sights:

Castle De Haar, Kasteellaan 1, Haarzuilens. Tel. 03407-1275.

Castle Doorn, Langbroekerweg 10, Doorn. Tel. 03430-12244.

Kaas en Museum Boerderij, Rottegatsteeg 6, Maarsbergen. Tel. 03498-1943.

Kees and Willie van de Dood, Piano Restoration, Wilhelminastraat 2A, Wijk-bij-Duurstede. Tel. 03435-76381.

Witches Weigh House, Leeuweringerstraat 2, Oudewater. Tel. 03486-3400

Hotels:

Leusden, ***Huize "Den Treek," Treekerweg 23, 3832 RS Leusden. Tel. 03498-1425.

Harmelen, ***Het Wapen van Harmelen, Dorpsstraat 14, 3481 EK Harmelen. Tel. 03483-1203.

Lage Vuursche, **Hotel De Kastanjehof, Kloosterlaan 1, 3749 AJ Lage Vuursche. Tel. 02156-8248.

Wijk-bij-Duurstede, ***Hotel De Oude Lantaarn, Markt 1, 396l BC Wijk-bij-Duurstede. Tel. 03435-71372.

Restaurants:

Wijk-bij-Duurstede, 't Schippershuys, Dijkstraat 5. Tel. 03435-71538.

Zeeland

Provincial VVV: Markt 65, Postbus 123, 4330 AC Middelburg. Tel. 01180-33000.

Museums and sights:

Delta-Expo, Neeltje Jans, Burgh-Haamstede. Tel. 01115-2702.

Roosevelt Study Center, Abdij 9, Postbus 6001, 4330 LA Middelburg. Tel. 01180-31356.

Zeeland Museum, Abdij 3, Middelburg. Tel. 01180-26655.

Hotels:

Middelburg, ****Hotel Arneville, Buitenruststraat 22, 4337 EH Middelburg. Tel. 01180-38456.

Middelburg, ***Hotel du Commerce, Loskade 1, 4331 HV Middelburg. Tel. 01180-36051.

The Wadden Isles

VVV North Holland for Texel, VVV Friesland for the other islands.

Birds & Birders Nature Tours, Postbus 737, 9700 AS Groningen. Tel. 050-145925.

Hotels:

Schiermonnikoog, ***Hotel Duinzicht, Badweg 17, 9166 ND Schiermonnikoog. Tel. 05195-1218.

Long-distance Rides

Stichtig Landelijk Fietsplatform, Bergstraat 6, 3811 NH Amersfoort. Tel. 033-653656.

Hotels:

Bergen aan Zee, ***Meyer Hotel, J. Kalffweg 4, 1865 AL. Tel. 02208-12488.

Brielle, ***Atlas Hotel, Nobelstraat 20, 3231 BC Brielle. Tel. 01810-13455.

Noordwijk, ***Hotel Zeerust, Quarles van Uffordstraat 103, 2202 NE Noordwijk. Tel. 01719-12723.

Four-day Cycling Events

NTFU, Landjuweel 11, Postbus 326, 3900 AH Veenendaal. Tel. 08385-21421/23319

Day Programs with the Railroads

Any NS station

Multiday VVV Cycling Arrangements

VVV offices

Covered Wagon Touring

VVV's Eindhoven en Kempenland, Stationsplein, Postbus 7, 5600 AA Eindhoven. Tel. 040-449231 (for multiday tours).

Onder de Groene Linde, Fam. A. van Och, Heikantstraat 23, Waalre. Tel. 04904-12723 (for day trips).

Cruising the Waterways

ANWB offices

Friesland Boating, De Tille 5, 8723 ER Koudum. Tel. 05142-2607.

L.J. Harri Nautical Bookstore, Prins Hendrikkade 94-95, 1012 AE Amsterdam. Tel. 020-6248052.

Zeilvaart Enkhuizen, Stationsplein 3, 1601 EN Enkhuizen. Tel. 02280-12424

Excursions on Foot

Stichting Lange-Afstand Wandelpaden, Bergstraat 6, Postbus 846, 3800 AV Amersfoort. Tel. 033-653660.

Bicycle Rental Addresses

Below is a *partial* list of *fietsverhuurbedrijven*, bicycle rental firms, that have both standard bicycles (single-speed bikes with coaster brake) and 3-speeds with handbrakes. Ask a VVV or your hotel for other possibilities. The great majority of rental shops in Holland rent out only standard bicycles, however. Because 3-speeds are more vulnerable than standard bikes, a 3-speed rental will usually cost you more than a standard. Phone, rather than write, to inquire about rentals and have a bicycle reserved for you.

Private rental shops may close Sundays and perhaps half a weekday. The NS station rental shops are open 7 days a week. They also operate a *fietsenstalling*, guarded bicycle parking facility, for a fee.

Drenthe

Assen: NS station. Tel. 05920-10424

Beilen: NS station. Tel. 05930-22260

Borger: Rijwielspeciaalzaak F. Egberts, Hoofdstraat 63 A. Tel. 05998-34224

Dwingeloo: Fietshandel Reiber, Brink 23. Tel. 05219-1326

Emmen: NS station. Tel. 05910-13731

Gasselte: Oosting Rijwielverhuur, Markeweg 7. Tel. 05999-64686

Norg: Stellingwerf Tweewielercentrum, Oosteind 25. Tel. 05928-13173

Ruinen:
Martens, Oosterstraat 4,Tel: 05221-1228

Vredenburg, Brink 39. Tel. 05221-1232

Flevoland

Lelystad: Rijwielhuis Cees Beers, Stationsplein 10. Tel. 03200-33122

Friesland

Koudum: Autobedrijf Kemker, Nieuweweg 10. Tel. 05142-1436

Leeuwarden: NS station. Tel. 058-139800

Gelderland

Arnhem: Roelofs Fietsspeciaalzaak, G.A. van Nispenstraat, Tel: 085-426014

Beekbergen: Ooms Tweewielers, Dorpsstraat 15 A, Tel: 05780-12362

Beesd: De Vaal, Voorstraat 53. Tel. 03458-1350

Ede-Wageningen: NS station. Tel. 08380-15957

Eerbeek: Gebr van den Brink, H.A. Grizellstraat 1. Tel. 08338-51734

Elburg: Koops, Beekstraat. Tel. 05250-4461

Epe: Ooms Tweewielers, Hoofdstraat 85. Tel. 05780-12362

Harderwijk: NS station. Tel. 03410-19927

Heelsum: Klein Tweewielers, Utrechtseweg 74. Tel. 08373-12426

Kootwijkerbroek: Tweewieler-centrum Jos. Westervelt, Veluweweg 194,Tel: 03423-1272

Lunteren: Groot Bramel, Dorpsstraat 31. Tel. 08388-2308

Nijmegen: NS station. Tel. 080-229618

Nunspeet: Rijwielhuis Hoegen, Stationslaan 79, Tel: 03412-58759

Putten: Tweewielers A. Kleijer, Huinerschoolweg 2. Tel. 03419-1237

Ruurlo: Fa. G.A. Mekking, Julianaplein 6-7. Tel. 05735-1227

Vierhouten: Alferink, Nunspeterweg 3. Tel. 05771-1204

Vorden: Hotel Bakker. Tel. 05752-1312

Zutphen: NS station. Tel. 05750-19327

Zeddam: Ariëns, Vinkwijkseweg 5A. Tel. 08345-1484

Groningen

Appingedam: Dijkema, Stationsstraat 9. Tel. 05960-22974

Groningen: NS station. Tel. 050-124174

Uithuizermeeden: Rijwielver-huur Idema, Hoofdstraat 146. Tel. 05954-12697

Limburg

Heerlen: NS station. Tel. 045-710601

Maastricht: NS station. Tel. 043-211100

Margraten: Fietsverhuurbedrijf Lemmerlijn, Rijksweg 3-5. Tel. 04458-1310

Mechelen: Tweewielcentrum, Hoofdstraat 55. Tel. 04455-1275

Roermond: NS station. Tel. 04750-18200

Valkenburg: Rijwielcentrum Oosterweg, Oosterweg 26. Tel. 04406-15338

Weert: Jansen's Verhuur. Tel. 04950-32986 (will deliver to hotel)

North Brabant

Asten: Tweewielers Wim van Veghel, Burg. Wijnenstraat 21. Tel. 04936-91355

Roosendaal: NS station. Tel. 01650-37228

North Holland

Alkmaar: NS station. Tel. 072-117907

Amsterdam: NS station Amstel. Tel. 020-6923584

Castricum: NS station. Tel. 02518-54035

Den Helder: NS station: Tel: 02230-19227

Egmond a/d Hoef: Karels, Herenweg 174. Tel. 02206-1226

Enkhuizen: Dekker Tweewielers, Nieuwstraat 2-6, Tel: 02280-12961

Hillegom: Jan Versteege, Hoofdstraat 116. Tel. 02520-15458

Nieuwe Niedorp: De Fietsen-man, Dorpsstraat 163, Tel: 02261-3322

Petten: Beukers Tweewielers, 1e v/d Banstraat 14, Tel: 02268-1367

Zaandam: NS station. Tel. 075-156593

Overijssel

Almelo: NS station. Tel. 05490-17837

Dalfsen: Fokkens, Prinsenstraat 16. Tel. 05293-1336

Enschede: NS station. Tel. 053-322792

Enter: Fa. Kornegoor, Dorpsstraat 94. Tel. 05478-1284

Holten: Tweewielerhuis Jan Stam, Oranjestraat 23, Tel: 05483-61779

IJhorst: Fa. Weemink, Heerenweg 42. Tel. 05224-1268

Nijverdal: Tweewielercentrum Aanstoot, Rijssensestraat 111. Tel. 05486-12717

Oldenzaal: Siemerink Tweewielers, Steenstraat 18, Tel: 05410-12077

Steenwijk: NS station. Tel. 05210-13991

Wierden: Van Ravenhorst Tweewieler, Kerkstraat 19. Tel. 05496-76013

Zwolle: NS station. Tel. 038-214598

South Holland

Alphen a/d Rijn: NS station. Tel. 01720-91400

Dordrecht: NS station. Tel. 078-146642

The Hague/Scheveningen: Du Nord, Keizerstraat 25-27, Tel: 070-3554060

Hook of Holland: Tweewielercentrum, near NS station Hoek van Holland Haven. Tel. 01747-82318

Leiden: NS station. Tel. 071-131304

Maassluis: NS station. Tel. 01899-16988

Noordwijk: Mooijekind, Schoolstraat 68. Tel. 01719-12826

Noordwijkerhout: Fa. Gijs van Dam, Havenstraat 22. Tel. 02523-72482

Schiedam: NS station. Tel. 010-4376772

Woerden: NS station. Tel. 03480-11656

Zwijndrecht: NS station. Tel. 078-125627

Utrecht

Bilthoven: Rijwielhandel A. Bakker, Soestdijkseweg Noord 302. Tel. 030-285538

Doorn: Rijwielhandel v/d Berg, Amersfoortseweg 57. Tel. 03430-12792

Rhenen: Rijwielspecialist Peter v/d Pijl, Molenstraat 35-37. Tel. 08376-12586

Zeeland

Goes: NS station. Tel. 01100-14170

Groede: Risseeuw Verhuur, Nieuwstraat 3. Tel. 01171-1462

Koudekerke/Dishoek: Rijwielhandel Kluijfhout, Kaapduinseweg 14A. Tel. 01185-2653

Middelburg: NS station. Tel. 01180-12178

Vlissingen: NS station. Tel. 01184-65951

Westkapelle: Rijwielshop Van Marion, Zuidstraat 99. Tel. 01187-2100

Wadden Isles

Ameland: Kiewiet, Reeweg 10 (near ferry), Martin Jansenstraat 6. Tel. 05191-2130

Schiermonnikoog: Schierfiets, Noorderstreek 32. Tel. 05195-31713

Fa. Soepboer, Paaslandweg 1,Tel: 05195-1636

Terschelling: Fa. Bakker, Lies 8. Tel. 05620-8823

Fa. Doeksen, Baaiduinen 36. Tel. 05620-8721

Knop Rijwielverhuur, Torenstraat 10-12. Tel. 05620-2052

Zeelen Rijwielverhuur, Lies 45. Tel. 05620-8309

Texel: Troost, Herenstraat 67, Den Hoorn. Tel. 02220-19213

Tweewielercentrum Kikkert, Badweg 19, De Koog. Tel. 02220-17215

Verhuurbedrijf Bruining, Nikadel 20, De Koog. Tel. 02220-17333

Vlieland: Jan Van Vlieland, Dorpsstraat 8. Tel. 05621-1509

Note on Changing Telephone Numbers

From time to time, the Dutch PTT (postal, telephone, and telegraph service) assigns an additional digit to selected telephone numbers. Consequently, any telephone number listed here or elsewhere may have changed when you get to Holland. Check at your hotel or at any PTT post office if you have reason to suspect the number you have may have been changed.

ANWB Map Legend Translation

Scale: 1:100,000 (1 centimeter on map equals 1 kilometer in field)

Autosnelweg	Freeway
Autosnelweg in aanleg	Freeway under construction
Hoofdroute, tweebaans	Main route, two-lane
Hoofdroute, eenbaans	Main route, one-lane
Hoofdroute in aanleg	Main route under construction
Belangrijke verbindingsweg, tweebaans	Important connecting road, two-lane
Belangrijke verbindingsweg, een-baans	Important connecting road, one-lane
Belangrijke verbindingsweg in aanleg	Important connecting road under construction
Weg van regionaal belang	Road of regional importance
Weg van plaatselijk belang	Road of local importance
Weg, verboden voor auto's	Road closed to cars
Weg met eenrichtingsverkeer	One-way road
Gedeeltelijk verharde weg	Partially paved road
Onverharde weg	Unpaved road
Dijk	Dike
Ontworpen weg	Projected road
Weg met vrijliggend(e) (brom) fietspad (en)	Road with roadside bicycle path(s), open to mopeds
Weg met vrijliggend(e) fietspad(en)	Road with roadside bicycle path, not open to mopeds.
(Brom) fietspad	Bikeway open to mopeds
Fietspad	Bikeway, cyclists only
Verhard toeristisch (brom) fietspad tenminste 2 m. breed	Paved touristic bikeway open to brommers, at least 2 meters wide
Weg, verboden voor (brom) fietsers	Road, closed to bicycles and brommers
Voetpad	Footpath
Schilderachtige route	Scenic route
Knooppunt Leidschendam	Name of major intersection
Afritbenaming autosnelwegen	Name of freeway exit
Nummering autosnelwegen	Number of freeway
Nummering Europaroutes	Number of Europaroute
Nummering niet-autosnelwegen Nederland	Number of highway in The Netherlands
Nummering niet-autosnelwegen Belgie	Number of highway in Belgium
Nummering "Bundesstrassen" Duitsland	Number of highway in Germany
Nummering autosnelwegen Duitsland	Number of freeway in Germany
Nummering stadsroutes	Number of city route

Afstand in km	Distance in kilometers
Tol; hek of afsluiting; helling	Toll; gate or barrier; grade
Spoorweg met station	Railroad with station
Idem P-R	Same, with Park & Ride
Goederenspoorweg	Freight railroad
Spoorweg onder weg	Railroad under road
Weg onder spoorweg	Road under railroad
Spoorweg kruist weg gelijkvloers	Level railway crossing
Brug, viaduct, tunnel	Bridge, viaduct, tunnel
Voetbrug	Foot bridge
Rivier, kanaal	River, canal
Beek	Brook
Veerdienst, niet voor auto's	Ferry service, not for cars
Veerdienst, ook voor auto's	Ferry service, also for cars (max. weight per vehicle 1,000 kg)
Kassengebied	Hothouse area

If scenic routes on the map are shown along unpaved roads, such roads are in many cases not suitable for motorized traffic.

Wherever possible, roadside bicycle paths are shown on the correct side of the road. But if there is a roadside bicycle path on both sides, it is shown only on one side.

ANWB kantoor	ANWB office
ANWB Wegenwachtstation	ANWB road service
ANWB wegwijzer of richtingsbord	ANWB road sign or directional sign
ANWB paddestoel	ANWB mushroom
Plaatselijke wegwijzer	Local road sign
Rijksgrens	National border
Provinciegrens	Provincial border
Bebouwde kom	Built-up area
Gehucht of buurtschap	Hamlet
Industrieterrein	Industrial area
Bijzonder gebouw	Noteworthy building
Gemeentehuis	Town or city hall
Kerk	Church
Bezienswaardige kerk	Church worth seeing
Klooster	Convent or monastery
Kapel of kruis	Chapel or crucifix
Begraafsplaats	Cemetery
ANWB kampeerterrein	ANWB campground
Kasteel, borg	Castle, mansion
Kasteel te bezichtigen	Castle open to public
Ruine	Ruins
Fabriek	Factory

Pompstation	Pumping station
Gemaal	Water level control station
Gedenkteken	Monument
Natuurreservaat	Nature preserve
Gemarkeerde wandelingen	Marked walks
Parkeer- of picknickplaats	Parking or picnic area
Bos	Forest, woods
Heide of woeste grond	Heath or uncultivated soil
Zand, duinen	Sand, dunes
Water	Water
Hunebed	Prehistoric burial chamber
(Voormalige) kolenmijn	(Former) coal mine
Molen	Windmill
Windturbine	Wind turbine
Waterradmolen	Waterwheel mill
Toren	Tower
Watertoren	Water tower
Brandtoren	Fire lookout
Vuurtoren	Lighthouse
Uitzicht	View
Uitzichtpunt	Vista point
Uitzichttoren	Vista tower
Dierenpark, hertenkamp	Zoo, deer park
Klokkestoel	Bell tower next to church
Eendenkooi	Duck pond
Sluis	Sluice
Openluchtzwembad	Open air swimming pool
Zwemgelegenheid	Opportunity for swimming
Dagrecreatieterrein	Day recreation terrain
Midgetgolf	Miniature golf
Golflinks	Golf course
Verkeersvliegveld	Commercial airport
Sport- of ander vliegveld	Sport or other airport
Zweefvliegterrein	Gliding terrain
Douanekantoor	Customs office
Ned.	Dutch
Belg.	Belgian
Duits	German
Landgoed, vrij toegankelijk	Estate open to public (free)
Landgoed, toegangskaart vereist	Estate open to public (admission charge)
Landgoed, niet toegankelijk	Estate not open to public
Mast/toren t.b.v. telecommunicatie	Telecommunication tower

APPENDIX D

Metric Conversion

In Holland, as indeed almost anywhere outside the United States, the metric system is used for all measures. The basic units are a meter for length, a gram for weight, a liter for volume, and a hectare for area, and the prefixes have the following meanings:

kilo-	1000	deci-	.1
hecto-	100	centi-	.01
deca-	10	milli-	.001

To convert these metric measures into the miles, pounds, gallons, and acres you are used to, travel with a pocket chart of such conversions. You can also work out conversions yourself as follows:

Distance
1 mile is approximately 1.6 kilometers
multiply miles by 1.6 to arrive at kilometers (10 miles = 16 kilometers) and multiply kilometers by 0.62 to arrive at miles (10 kilometers = 6.2 miles).

Weight
2.2 pounds equal 1 kilogram
divide pounds by 2.2 to arrive at kilograms (10 pounds = 4.6 kilograms) and multiply kilograms by 2.2 to arrive at pounds (10 kilograms = 22 pounds).

Volume
1 U.S. gallon is approximately 3.8 liters
multiply the gallons by 3.8 to arrive at liters (10 gallons = 38 liters) and divide the liters by 3.8 to arrive at gallons (10 liters = 2.7 gallons).

1 imperial gallon is approximately 4.5 liters
multiply the gallons by 4.5 to arrive at liters (10 gallons = 45 liters) and divide the liters by 4.5 to arrive at gallons (10 liters = 2.2 gallons).

Area
1 acre is almost 0.4 hectares
multiply acres by 0.4 to arrive at hectares (10 acres = 4 hectares) and divide hectares by 0.4 to arrive at acres (10 hectares = 25 acres).

Temperature
$°C = \frac{5}{9} (°F — 32)$
A pocket diary may have a drawing of a thermometer with Celsius on one side and Fahrenheit on the other side. If no such handy tool is available, multiply the Celsius degrees by $\frac{9}{5}$ and add 32 (or, as a rough approximation, multipy by 2 and add 30) to arrive at the equivalent Fahrenheit reading; or subtract 32 from the Fahrenheit degrees and multiply by $\frac{5}{9}$ (or as a rough approximation, subtract 30 and divide by 2) to arrive at the equivalent Celsius temperature. The freezing point, 32° on the Fahrenheit scale, is 0°C.

The Netherlands and its provinces

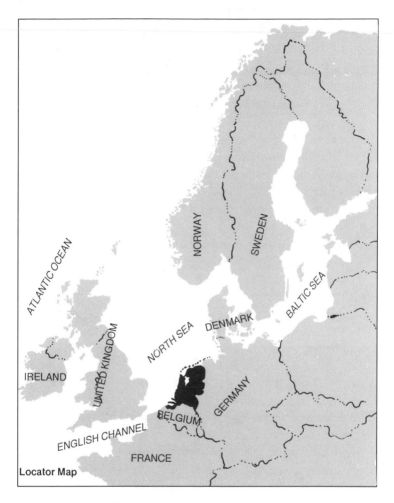

The Netherlands in relation to other European countries

In the Holland section of a travel bookstore, and in the travel section of some general bookstores, you are likely to find English-language copies of long-published and regularly updated travel guides that bear names like Baedeker, Fielding, Fodor, Frommer, and Lonely Planet.

Also present on the shelf will probably be the three standard guides from France: the Michelin "Green Guide," entitled *Netherlands*, its companion "Red Guide" on hotels and restaurants, entitled *Holland, Belgium and Luxembourg*, and the "Blue Guide" *Holland*. The last is considered more academic, giving more details on history and art than the "Green Guide," but is not updated as often.

Other guidebooks to Holland include the Insight guide *The Netherlands* (APA Publications, Singapore) and *The Real Guide – Holland, Belgium, Luxembourg* (Prentice Hall General Reference). Among specialized guidebooks may be *Slow Walks in Amsterdam*, a book in the Perennial Library (HarperCollins, New York) and, under the same imprint, *Of Dutch Ways* with lots of background on The Netherlands and the Dutch.

Travelers interested in learning the Dutch language may want to reach for the pocket-size Berlitz English-Dutch/ Dutch-English dictionary.

You'll also find some of the above titles in Holland—at places like Schiphol airport, specialized bookstores mentioned in Appendix A of this book, and some general bookstores. Large hotels may sell English-language travel guides in their gift shops.

Available from specialized bookstores or the ENFB Cyclists Association (Havenstraat 13, Postbus 2150, 3440 DD Woerden, Tel: 03480-23119) is *Hiking and biking through the Netherlands*. This lightweight passport-size booklet lists addresses for inexpensive overnights at campsites, in youth hostels and private homes, and for ferry services, including pedestrian ferries. Since ordering from your home will entail high bank charges to purchase the required guilders check, you may want to wait until you are in the country.